CVs and Job Applications

Judith Leigh is a history graduate from the University of London. She has held a variety of management and HR posts in commercial and non-commercial organizations. She currently works for a national heritage charity.

One Step Ahead . . .

The *One Step Ahead* series is for all those who want and need to communicate more effectively in a range of real-life situations. Each title provides up-to-date practical guidance, tips, and the language tools to enhance your writing and speaking.

Series Editor: John Seely

Titles in the series

CVs and Job Applications	Judith Leigh
Editing and Revising Text	Jo Billingham
Essays and Dissertations	Chris Mounsey
Giving Presentations	Jo Billingham
Law in Everyday Life	John Seely
Organizing and Participating in Meetings	Judith Leigh
Presenting Numbers, Tables, and Charts	Sally Bigwood and Melissa Spore
Publicity, Newsletters, and Press Releases	Alison Baverstock
Punctuation	Robert Allen
Spelling	Robert Allen
Words	John Seely
Writing Bids and Funding Applications	Jane Dorner
Writing for the Internet	Jane Dorner
Writing Reports	John Seely

Acknowledgements

My thanks to Reed.co.uk for permission to quote from their report on on-line applications survey and reproduce screen shots of their web site.

I am indebted to the friends and colleagues who took the time and trouble to give me their experience and advice, especially Jim Blakelock, Eira Gibson, Mark and Gill Ellis, Jackie Till, and Kate Bell. Their perspectives on the job hunt, as candidates, recruiters, and resource providers, were invaluable.

My thanks to all my HR colleagues, especially: Judy Kopp and her colleagues at Covent Garden Bureau, Simon Downing at the National Trust, Julian Yew of Hextall Erskine, Roger Fagg of Birkbeck College, University of London, and not forgetting Chris Harrington-Benton for emailing all the HR jokes.

CVs and Job Applications

Judith Leigh

Cartoons by Beatrice Baumgartner-Cohen

For my good friends at the Historic Churches Preservation Trust, especially James, with the hope that you will never need this book.

OXFORD UNIVERSITY PRESS

Great Clarendon Street, Oxford OX2 6DP

Oxford University Press is a department of the University of Oxford.
It furthers the University's objective of excellence in research, scholarship,
and education by publishing worldwide in
Oxford New York
Auckland Bangkok Buenos Aires Cape Town Chennai
Dar es Salaam Delhi Hong Kong Istanbul Karachi Kolkata
Kuala Lumpur Madrid Melbourne Mexico City Mumbai Nairobi
São Paulo Shanghai Taipei Tokyo Toronto

Oxford is a registered trade mark of Oxford University Press
in the UK and in certain other countries

Published in the United States
by Oxford University Press Inc., New York

© Judith Leigh 2004

The moral rights of the author have been asserted
Database right Oxford University Press (maker)

First published 2004

British Library Cataloguing in Publication Data
Data available

Library of Congress Cataloging in Publication Data
Data available

ISBN 0-19-860614-1

10 9 8 7 6 5 4 3 2 1

Typeset by Footnote Graphics Ltd, Warminster, Wiltshire
Printed by Ashford Colour Press Ltd, Gosport, Hampshire

Contents

1 Setting the scene

*Get the job
you want by
telling the
people you
want to work
with what
they need to
know.*

Introduction

This book aims to help you get the job you want by telling the
people you want to work with what they need to know.

This is the essence of what successful CVs and application
forms are all about. They present the information that an
employer needs to make a balanced judgement about your
suitability for work with them. Although very few employers
would offer you a job solely on the basis of your CV or
application form, they are vital to gain you an interview. A
badly presented or targeted CV or application will ensure that
you never reach that stage.

Just as your career develops, so too should your CV.
Throughout the book, tips on how to amend a CV to give a
good pen portrait of yourself as you move up the career ladder
or switch job direction are included.

Making sure you follow up a good CV with a good interview is
essential and therefore interview techniques are also covered.

This is a book of *guidelines* and although there are a few rules
that everyone should follow—such as checking the spelling on
a CV or application form—you will probably find a
mix'n'match approach to its advice is best. Use the tips to find
a basic system that works for you and develop this core system
to suit your individual style and aspirations.

Using this book

Part A takes you through the various steps of the job hunt, from initial research to preparing for an interview. Each chapter starts with a general introduction to the topic covered followed by more specific descriptions and suggestions on the various points you will need to consider when building up your skills as a successful job applicant.

Chapters 2 and 3 deal with the preparation you need to do before you apply for any post. Chapters 4 to 8 deal with the different formats of applying for a job from CVs to online applications. Chapter 9 discusses interview techniques. Chapter 10 gives a brief overview of things you need to think about before confirming acceptance of a job, such as terms and conditions of employment. Chapter 11 is devoted to troubleshooting. Just as machinery sometimes goes wrong, sometimes a career can run into trouble. This chapter gives some hints about turning the situation round and making a fresh start.

In the margins, you will find boxes giving 'quick tips' and warnings—the 'do's and 'don't's of applying for a job. Also in the margins are a variety of quotations about work and finding a job. Some may make you smile, but if you find yourself in sympathy with too many of the negative views, perhaps it is time to plan a new strategy: either to your attitude to work or your approach to finding a job.

Quick tip
You will also find more help and advice on the One Step Ahead web pages (www.askoxford. com).

Part B contains the flow charts, checklists, and examples referred to in Part A. Cross-references to other chapters or items in Part B are given in the margins of Part A.

This book is about applying for jobs in the UK but a list of reference sources to help you apply for jobs elsewhere in the world is given in Part B.

See Part B, page 141.

Introducing four applicants

A CV is not a static item but grows as your experience and skills grow.

A CV is not a static item that once written, never needs revisiting. Similarly, the way you complete a job application form will change as your experience grows. The aim of this book is to give you constructive help, whatever your degree of job experience or at whatever level you are at on the career ladder.

For this reason, throughout the book, examples of CVs and job applications are given based on the experience of four people who are at different stages in their career. Below are brief biographies of the four, one of which hopefully will hopefully equate roughly to your current career situation.

- *Joe* is 18 and has recently finished a BTECH, and is wondering how to start his career. He hasn't any strong feelings about which field to work in, other than the fact that he does not like a formal working environment and, in the future, he would like to be involved in creative work.

- *Kashmira* is in her late 20s and has been working for five years since graduating from university. She is beginning to feel bored in her current job and wants to make the first move into a management role. She isn't sure how to communicate her readiness to break into management from a junior post.

- *Hannah* is in her late 30s and has had a break from working while her children were young. Now that her children are all at school, she wants to get back to work. She had five years' work experience before she took her career break. Her last post was team supervisor in a call centre.

- *Richard* is in his late 40s. He has been working for the same company for the last ten years and has progressed through various roles to be currently the Product Director. Due to a planned merger, Richard knows his post will be made redundant in the next few months. He has decided to take a positive approach to this event as he feels this might be an ideal opportunity to change his career completely.

The building blocks of the job hunt

Successful job applications are built using four 'building blocks': Research, Target, Prepare, and Communicate. These four blocks are the load, aim, and fire sequence which will land you the job you want.

The building blocks of job applications

■ **Research** covers the work you need to do to find out about yourself, the job, and the company.

■ **Target** means focusing your CV or job application to suit the demands of the job or conversely finding a company which best suits the skills, knowledge, and experience you have.

■ **Prepare** involves checking your CV or your application; practising for the interview.

■ **Communicate** covers writing your CV, application form, and covering letter, and giving a good interview.

Quick tip
The point to remember is that Communicate always comes last. The temptation for many job candidates is to jump from reading a job advert straight to Communicate.

2 Groundwork

A successful application is usually the result of good initial groundwork by the candidate.

Introduction

A successful application is usually the result of good initial groundwork by the candidate. Thinking back to the four building blocks outlined in Chapter 1, this groundwork includes the blocks of:

■ **Research**

■ **Target**

■ **Prepare.**

This chapter concentrates on the Research aspect of making a job application. Research is a vital part of any application and it falls into three parts:

■ researching yourself

■ researching the job you want to do

■ researching the organization you want to work for.

Researching yourself is a much bigger topic than can be covered in depth in this book. The first section of this chapter gives you pointers to get started but you will probably find it useful to look at other books dedicated to this area as well.

Researching jobs and organizations has never been easier thanks to the proliferation of information on the internet. Setting the guidelines to find the information you need is discussed in the last two sections of this chapter.

See Part B, Further resources, page 109.

Researching yourself: what do you want to do?

Before you start to think of applying for a job, you need to do some important research: research on YOU.

Microsoft Software has a catchphrase, 'Where do you want to go today?' You need to make that decision each time you decide to make a change in your career, whether you are at the start of your working life, thinking of moving to a different company, and especially if you are considering a complete change of direction. The key questions you need to answer are:

✔ *Do!*

decide what you want to do before starting your job hunt.

- What am I interested in?

- What are my skills and experiences?

- What are the best and worst aspects of my current job?

- What are my career aims in the short, medium, and long term?

✘ *Don't!*

apply for any job that you think you could do: find a personal interest or career aim involved with it.

The following are examples of answers to these questions by two of the four people introduced in Chapter 1: Joe and Richard. First, Joe.

See Chapter 1, page 8.

Interests

- Music: blues, jazz.

- Sport: especially football and athletics.

- People: like meeting new people from lots of different backgrounds.

- Always wanted to travel.

Joe

Quick Tip
Be specific about your interests: don't just say 'sport' but which sports, not just 'music' but what type of music. This will become important when discussing how to build the 'hinterland' of your CV.

Skills and experience

- Four weeks' work experience at local solicitors' office giving general administrative assistance.

- Good IT skills.

Best and worst aspects

■ At solicitors' office, liked learning new things (the telephone switchboard was the best of all).

■ Didn't like the very structured and formal atmosphere.

■ At college, enjoyed the IT modules best.

■ At college, liked the report-writing modules least.

Career aims

■ Short term: to get a job!

■ Mid term: don't know—being promoted?

■ Long term: something creative?

Joe's responses are fairly typical for someone starting out: he has not had enough time to look round the job market and see what interests him or what parts of a job will be the best or most boring for him. Joe needs to try to find a job that ties into his interests but does not force him into a particular channel. When you start your working life, look for jobs which will give you:

Being an MP is the sort of job all working-class parents want for their children— clean, indoors and no heavy lifting.

Diane Abbott, *Independent*

■ **core skills in the chosen broad area of your career**
For example if you feel your career will be based in an office, look for an administrative post which will cover office basics such as computers, using a telephone system, and dealing with the public. If you are looking for a career in the catering trade, look for a post that will show you kitchen basics such as food preparation, hygiene, and use of different types of kitchen equipment.

■ **opportunities for training**
An ideal job goes on teaching you new things all the time, no matter where you are in your career. Companies which are not interested in promoting this aspect of work rarely have a good track record with their staff. Training may be structured, with day release or evening courses included and even paid for, or on-the-job training with regular in-house sessions.

a career structure

A sense of progression helps your motivation. Multinationals, the Civil Service, local Councils and academic institutions will have structured systems leading you up a career ladder (or crossing between different areas, say from retail to marketing). Smaller companies will have a looser structure, relying either on new work coming in to drive the process of promotion or staff leaving and opening up opportunities for others. Which structure appeals to you will depend on your personality. However, look out for danger signs in firms where people seem to be 'stuck' in a role and are frustrated by this.

In a hierarchy every employee tends to rise to his level of incompetence.

Laurence J. Peter, *The Peter Principle*

Joe has two or three 'ideal' careers open to him.

- Working as an administrator with a music company: an office job, but the atmosphere will be informal compared to a solicitors. There will be lots of different people to meet and Joe will have the opportunity to learn about the music industry from the bottom up.

Quick Tip
There is nothing wrong in finding your 'niche' in a company and staying put at that level: HR managers are usually desperate to find stayers at all levels.

- A post in a sports venue or in a company sponsoring sporting events. Posts do turn up with football clubs, but Joe would need more work experience before he could compete with the dozens of other applicants. It may be worth Joe's time contacting 'his' team and asking what qualifications and experience would be expected. Joe can then map a career and training which will fit him for the role. For example, if the club wants staff who have experience of particular software, Joe could look for companies who use this software or start saving to pay for private training in his spare time.

- A role with a company that has a creative aim; media, designers, architects, printers. Starting from scratch in a firm where training is encouraged and staff are promoted through experience would be helpful.

One of the most popular interview questions is 'What career plans do you have?' Plan your answer before you've even applied for a job.

These are 'ideal' careers, but if Joe starts a flexible career plan now, with these jobs in mind, he will have a career direction and be able to present himself much more dynamically on his CV and at interview.

Quick Tip
Memberships of an organization demonstrate that you are actively involved in your interests and have made a certain commitment to supporting them.

Quick Tip
At this stage of your research, don't write detailed notes of every single skill you possess: do this section quickly so that the things you write down are the ones that immediately suggest themselves to you as your strongest skills.

Richard

The second example is Richard.

Interests

■ Countryside and the environment—member of Ramblers' Association, National Trust, Worldwide Fund for Nature, Wildfowl & Wetlands Trust.

■ Family—two daughters and one son (all in teens); occasional fostering for local authority.

Skills

■ 20 years' experience in design and production; 10 years' management experience, including project management, costing and budget control, reporting to directors.

■ Good verbal and written communication skills; experienced in writing and making presentations.

■ Good at putting teams together and leading them.

■ 8 O-levels, 3 A-levels, degree in mechanical engineering.

Short-term career aims (now to 1 year)

■ Depending on redundancy package, take training course in charity administration or fundraising with aim to finding job in charity which matches personal interests.

Mid-term career aims (1 year to 3 years)

■ Having completed training, look for suitable post in a charity, and gain experience.

Long-term career aims (3 years onwards)

■ Possibly move into political lobbying for charities.

Richard is, strangely enough, in a similar position to Joe. The end of his current job leaves him with a completely open field so that his career could go in a variety of directions. Where Richard differs from Joe is that he has a good idea of the sector he wants to work in: charity. Charities are interested in managers with solid experience and the range of skills Richard can demonstrate—his knowledge of production operations, his good communication skills in meetings and presentations. Richard also has a useful number of personal interests which demonstrate his commitment to a number of charities.

Where Joe has the edge on Richard is that Richard's career has been in the same area for a long time which means he has things to 'unlearn'. For example, Richard may find it a shock to move back into a formal learning environment as he retrains and then moves from the commercial world into the charity sector. Out go the expense account lunches and annual bonuses: in come stringent financial restraints and a hands-on approach to all aspects of a job. Before setting off on his chosen course, Richard would need to consider:

■ **finances**
It is essential when switching careers to be prepared for your salary to plummet in the short term and work out how you will cover the shortfall. Exactly how much do you need to live on and, from this, what salary must you earn?

■ **training**
What courses will give you the knowledge you need? What do they cost, where are they run, and when do they start? Do you need a minimum qualification to join? Having a vague idea about retraining will be a disaster if you find out that you missed the starting date of the only course by a month and have to wait a year before it starts again.

■ **having a 'taster'**
If, like Richard, you have never worked in a charity, it would be worth having a trial before you switch careers. Charities are usually delighted to have volunteers, though it is likely that voluntary work will be of a lower grade than you might be used to—anything from stuffing envelopes to hacking down undergrowth. Similarly, if you want to change roles in business, use your contacts inside and outside your current company, friends and relatives, to see if you can 'shadow' someone in the job you are interested in for a few days. Learning what it is like from the inside can be an eye-opener.

Are you a member of a charitable or professional organization? How much do you know about the way they work? Take the time to read the annual report and accounts, check out the web sites and see how they operate. Attend local meetings if possible and see if you can add to your skills and knowledge from the discussion.

It is important to give yourself a time frame, and revisit your plan every six months to alter it as circumstances change. Your plan is not set in stone, but giving yourself some deadlines can help motivate you to achieve it.

What's missing?

After you have thought through the key questions, it is worth getting a second opinion on your answers. Both Joe and Richard have missed important parts out of their personal profiling: Joe has not listed his BTECH under *Skills and experience*; Richard has forgotten that he has committed himself to a sponsored cycle ride for one month in his *Short-term career aims*. Another view of each of their situations would have been very helpful.

Ask a family member, a trusted friend, or work colleague to write their own list of what they think your strengths and weaknesses are. It is best if they do this very quickly—ask them to spend no more than ten minutes writing single words under the headings *Strengths* and *Weaknesses*. This way you will get a more honest response, but this is why it is important that you do this exercise with someone you trust. Work colleagues must be reliable enough not to share their views and your intentions to change jobs with the rest of the company. If you know someone who is in a similar situation to you, this could be a mutually useful exercise. If Richard could identify another manager in a different department who is also expecting to be made redundant, then they could work together on this project.

You could be very surprised at the feedback you gain. For example, Joe's best friend puts the word 'shy' under Joe's weaknesses, although Joe thinks that he gets on well with people. Joe gets on well with *friends*, but he tends to be shy when he meets people face-to-face— hence his enjoyment of switchboard work at the solicitors. Joe will need to spend some time debating if he should work on this weakness or look for a job where he has less contact with strangers.

Maybe meeting people isn't my strong point...

Richard's wife has reminded him that he *did* do some voluntary work about ten years ago: it would be interesting for Richard to work out why he had forgotten about this. Was it very boring or did he have so much fun that it didn't feel like work?

A totally independent view can also be beneficial. Don't forget to make use of your local careers advisory service. Universities often offer their own graduates free careers advice, plus workshops on interviewing skills and CV writing. Large companies implementing a redundancy programme will also usually offer employees sessions with external consultants.

Do!

use your local careers advice centre.

If you are at managerial level, consider using a dedicated consultancy. These are not recruitment consultancies and work in a quite different way, analysing your career aspirations and experience in rigorous detail and coaching you on a one-to-one basis to improve your interviewing and presentation skills. Such consultancies frequently have access to unadvertised jobs and will actively look for appropriate posts for you. However, they are expensive: you will probably have to pay a fee and if the agency places you in a job, you may have to agree to pay the agency a percentage of your first year's salary. You must therefore make your own careful investigation of the integrity and track record of the company you select.

Don't!

use a career agency that charges you a fee without careful preliminary research.

A word of caution

Self research can be quite painful on occasion. You will find most respected self-help books will advise you that this can be an exhausting process which can throw up all sorts of long forgotten troubles and angsts. Take the process slowly and if you decide to seek outside help, look for a counsellor with the relevant qualifications from a recognized body. Companies offering psychometric testing—a form of aptitude, ability, and career development testing—should be registered with the British Psychological Society, www.bps.org.uk.

Researching the job

A rose by any other name would smell as sweet . . .

William Shakespeare

Give yourself time to get the full details before applying for any job, no matter how straightforward it may seem.

As you read through an application pack, make notes for yourself. What seems most important in the role so that you can focus your application on this aspect? What is not clear in the pack, which you could ask about at interview?

See also page 24.

See Part B, page 110, for an example of a job description.

What's in a name?

When you read through job adverts, the purpose of some jobs seems obvious—a PA, a baker, a police officer, a teacher are all instantly recognizable roles. But what about a communications administrator, an archaeology commissions manager, or an SRB5 project officer? There are also roles which have different meanings to different companies: distributions manager, site manager, director. The fact is that all roles, even the seemingly straightforward ones such as baker and teacher, are unique.

This is why many job advertisements carry the crucial phrase 'full job description available' or 'call for application pack'. It may be tempting to fire off your CV to a company as soon as you have read the advert, but the opportunity is being handed to you on a plate to find out what the job really entails. Without doing so, you will probably find later that you applied incorrectly: either because you would not have been interested in the job if you knew what it involved or because you failed to target your application correctly.

Comprehensive application packs will consist of:

■ job description

■ person specification

■ company information

■ department information

■ information about the recruitment procedure

■ information about the terms and conditions of employment

■ application form.

The *job description* will tell you what the responsibilities and tasks are that make up the job. As a general rule, the shorter and simpler the description, the less responsibility the post has in a company hierarchy. Descriptions of management posts may run to several pages and include details of targets or policy to be implemented.

A *person specification* describes the organization's perfect candidate. It may be divided into qualifications, skills, work experience, and these sections will be subdivided into 'essential' and 'desirable'. Essential items are those you must have; desirable items will give you an additional edge.

See Part B, page 111, for an example of a person specification.

You need to read 'between the lines' of job descriptions and person specifications, to spot hidden challenges in a job. Emphasis, for example, on managing client relations in the description of a job which does not appear to be primarily about client relations may indicate the company is in trouble in this area. If a person specification concentrates on skills and experience at working with a 'hard-pressed' team you may deduce that the team has had difficulties or awkward people are involved.

Quick Tip
Keep copies of person specifications of jobs you would have liked to apply for or companies you would have liked to work for if you had had all the essential items listed. Use these as guidelines for future career development: how can you mould your career to give you these skills or experience?

Department information will give you a notion of what the department's immediate and long-term aims are. Again, look for the hidden clues. 'After a period of change, the department is now aiming to provide its users with high standards of service' means that staff morale may be very low following a serious shake up, or may be very high thanks to a dynamic manager who has revived a stagnant department. Look for other clues to decide which is the correct solution: has this vacancy come about as the result of a promotion or someone leaving? What does the organizational information tell you? What have you read in the press?

The details on *recruitment procedure* may also help you to determine if this is the right role for you. Everyone expects to be interviewed for a job, but if the procedure also involves going to an assessment centre for a day of tests, group exercises, and panel interviews, you may decide this is not for you. Don't be put off by such procedures; they are typical for fast track executive or senior management roles and if you have the chance, try the system once at least.

Terms and conditions of employment are dealt with in Chapter 10. At this point, you need to check that what is being offered suits you.

Where to look

Researching a job you have already spotted being advertised is easy: what about finding a job to research to start with?

An advert in the local or national press is often the starting point for a job search. Some national newspapers have become the accepted places to look for certain types of job, for example:

■ *Guardian*: jobs at all levels in the media, arts and museums, social services, education, local government, charities, IT, and a general section dedicated to a raft of unusual and blue chip companies. Good career guide section also carried, with descriptions of jobs, what qualifications and experience they require, details of companies, and their 'rating' as a place of employment.

■ *The Times*: posts at all levels of graduate entry, executive and higher management in blue chip companies, charities, local and national government, health service, law. Selection of experienced and junior administration and secretarial posts. Also publishes the *Times Educational Supplement* which covers educational and teaching posts.

■ *Daily Telegraph*: particularly strong in engineering and operational management posts.

All the above newspapers also run comprehensive online job listings.

Free magazines and newspapers are usually paid for by their advertisers, so they will have a wide range of agency vacancies for anything from a junior secretary to a security guard.

Trade publications advertise jobs within the sector covered by the publication. If you're not sure what trade publications there are for the area you want to look for a job in, ask your local reference library or your newsagent for help. Libraries and newsagents have comprehensive catalogues of all available publications. Newsagents will be able to order you a copy and libraries will be able to give you contact details of how to subscribe direct to a publication.

Make a note of which days adverts for your chosen job sector appear in which papers and set a diary reminder to yourself to buy them on those days.

Website addresses for these newspapers' on-line recruitment services are in Part B, Further resources, page 139.

See Part B, Further resources, page 139, for a list of some of the better known trade press publications.

Quick Tip
Keep a note of the name and contact details of agencies who seem to be advertising the type of jobs you are interested in.

Recruitment agencies

Recruitment agencies divide roughly into two halves:

- those which deal with jobs from very junior positions up to lower management level in one or more sectors. At these agencies, you register with the agency and they will check your skills and experience against jobs on their register to find a match. Registering with an agency will give you the opportunity to hear about jobs which are not advertised elsewhere. The better agencies will be keen to help you achieve your career aims and will take the time to give you advice and guidance: listen to it.

- those which deal with middle and senior management posts. These consultancies have well-established relations with a number of companies or are known for finding and placing a certain type of manager in a given sector. They do not have a registration system for candidates and work on the basis of advertising in the press and sometimes on their web site. Applications are then filtered by the agency before being passed to the company they have been retained by.

  These consultancies also head-hunt, by knowing the senior or specialized personnel at companies in their field. They will approach someone who they think fits a profile and will open negotiations with them. Once a consultancy finds you a post, they will often remain in contact with you and be open to approaches when you are looking for a new post.

 Do!

make sure an agency knows what type of job you want and what your skills and experience are to avoid being sent for interviews which are not suitable.

The golden rule when job searching with an agency is to ensure that the agency knows what type of job you want and what your skills and experience are. You can achieve this by filling in any registration forms honestly and building up a relationship with your consultant by giving feedback after each interview the agency arranges for you. This avoids you attending interviews which are not suitable. Irrelevant interviews are irritating for you, the agency, and the employer.

If the agency persists in sending you details of inappropriate jobs, you need to explain this to them and if this brings no results, ask to be taken off their books.

Internet advertising

There has been a boom in job advertising on the internet in recent years. There are three types of sites to look at:

See Chapter 8 for details of how to apply on-line.

Keep a diary of dates when companies you are keen to work for will be opening up their application procedures, e.g. for graduate and college leaver entry.

The web site address of a company can often tell you which country the company is based in. The suffix .uk will tell you this is a UK-based company, the suffix .au is for Australia, .nz for New Zealand. This means you can save time by ignoring those search results for companies based outside the country you wish to work in.

- *dedicated recruitment sites*, such as Monster, TopJobs, and WorkThing, carry adverts from a whole range of companies and organizations. They also offer the opportunity to register your CV on the site so that employers looking for people with your skills, experience, and qualifications will be sent your CV when a match crops up.

- *recruitment agencies' web sites*: nearly every recruitment agency now runs its own web site with details of the vacancies they have on their books. Besides giving you the opportunity to scan current opportunities, you can again register your CV and can opt to receive automatic emails when a new job comes up which matches your profile. These web sites are also useful to filter out agencies which do not cover your chosen career area, saving you a wasted journey to register in person at their office.

- *company web sites*: many companies advertise their own vacancies on their web sites. These pages will also give you vital data about what information the company needs from you to consider your application. If a company states that it is not currently considering applications, respect this but there is no harm in sending an email or making a phone call to the HR department to ask when they anticipate reopening their application procedure.

It may seem these sites are only useful if you know which company you are interested in working for and can search for its web site directly. However, remember that doing an internet search on the area of business you are interested in will produce lists of companies which work in that field. For example, if you are interested in being a sales rep in the electrical industry, a search on the key words 'electrical sales' will produce a list of companies selling electrical goods. If your search produces a daunting result list of thousands of entries, narrow your search by adding additional words such as 'jobs', 'careers', or 'opportunities'. You can also focus your search by geographical area, by adding 'north east' or 'Bedfordshire' to 'electrical sales'. Be prepared to take your time over a productive internet search. Ideally, do not combine it with registering for jobs: do your company research in one phase, as described in the next section, and your application registration in another phase, so that the Research block does not get muddled with the Communicate block.

Networking

'Networking' to find job vacancies is a long-established procedure and carries good and bad connotations. The concept of it not being *what* you know but *who* you know that gets you the job can be very frustrating, if you feel you are not part of the 'right' network. What you need to remember is that you have your own network which starts with family, then friends, then past and present colleagues. A few phone calls or an email to everyone you know asking them to keep an eye out for openings often produces unexpected returns. As you rise up the career ladder, your network should get bigger and perhaps more specialized as your career settles into one area. This is the reason why senior managers get head-hunted from one company to another: they have been dealing and working with similar—perhaps even the same—people for long enough for their reputation and skills in a certain area to be well-known and attractive to another company. Forget the 'old school tie' network: any reputable company has scrapped this recruitment principle years ago.

 Do!

think twice about working with or for someone you know as a friend. While they may be great company for a night out, do you really want to work day in and day out with that person?

 Don't!

be afraid to ask your friends for any news they hear about opportunities.

l don't think l'm much good at networking

Researching the company

The final part of your programme of research is to find out about the company (or any type of organization) to which you want to apply.

If you have received an application pack from a company, this is the stage where you need to consider the company information sent with the pack. Such information may consist of:

Quick Tip
Make notes for yourself as you read through company information. What are the key factors that should be included in your application? Is there anything that is not fully explained which could be discussed at interview?

See Part B, page 138, for resources on company structures.

- a **publicity leaflet**: only useful up to a certain extent because it is aimed at customers and will give a limited number of facts.

- a **mission statement**: a short statement of the company's aims and aspirations, which may also give a break down of the current situation of the company and future targets.

- information on the **company structure**: often given in the form of departmental diagrams showing the management structure. From these diagrams you should be able to deduce if this is an organization with a loose, flat structure where most employees have the chance to make direct contributions to the strategy and operation of the company. Alternatively, there may be a more rigid, hierarchical structure with layers of staff at different grades. You need to go back to the research on yourself and decide which structure will best suit your preferred style of working.

- **annual reports and accounts**: the crucial parts of the report and accounts to look at are the chairperson's statement, the balance sheet, and the profit and loss account. The chair's statement will give you valuable hints about what the company has achieved over the past twelve months and what is intended for the next year. Have any weaknesses been identified or are performance strengths being built on? Do not be automatically deterred by a statement which refers to redundancies or cutting back *as long as it has already happened*: companies which have already taken action to resolve problems are in a stronger position than a company which has a vague statement from the chair which tells you nothing. In the accounts, compare the figures for the current year to the previous year (which will also be in the accounts). Does the chair's statement explain major differences? If there has been a big jump in realizing capital assets, this may be a warning that the company is having to raise money to cover lost customers. However, it could also be to finance the purchase of up-to-date technology or investment in new areas: either way, the chair's statement should explain this.

■ **latest newsletter**: again, if this is a newsletter for customers (this includes members of a membership organization), it will give you the positive aspects of a company and you need to be wary of accepting it fully at face value. However, the fact that an organization cares enough for its customers to keep them updated should give it extra marks.

Larger organizations often have a staff newsletter as well as a customer newsletter. This can be useful in giving you a feel for the 'culture' of the company: does it concentrate on sales targets or stories about how well the staff football team did?

Quick Tip
The further you progress up the career ladder, the more important a careful examination of the annual report and accounts becomes. You may be expected to give your appraisal at interview of the company's financial situation and how you can contribute to it. Your benefits package may consist of shares in the company: check that they are worth the paper they are written on before accepting.

Stay informed

Retain the application pack a company sends you. If you are invited to an interview, rereading this information will form part of your interview preparation (see Chapter 9). You will find it annoying if you are invited to interview only to discover you no longer have the company information and the recruitment manager will not be impressed if you ask for it again.

If you are not invited to interview or are not offered the job after an interview but are still interested in the company, keep the pack for future applications. It would be interesting to compare what the company sends out in six months' or a year's time, and will gain you marks at interview if you can demonstrate an ongoing interest in and knowledge of the company. Think of setting up a quick reference system which focuses on key points such as the names of managers, products, income, number of customers (or members), any plans for expansion or new ventures.

Do it yourself research

If the company does not send you any information, you will
need to do some research yourself.

■ Check the company web site

This will give you a company overview and other clues. For
example, what sort of web site is it? A plain or dull site
speaks volumes, just as an attractive, well-planned site does.
If the information on the web site is out-of-date does this
point to a company which starts new projects, like a web
presence, enthusiastically, but loses interest after a while?

■ Ask the company

Applicants are sometimes reluctant to ask the company
itself for more details in case they appear ignorant. It would
be very unusual for any recruitment manager to think this
and much more likely for them to be immediately interested
in a candidate who shows initiative.

■ Ask the agency

If you are being sent on an interview by a recruitment
agency, they should be able to brief you properly about both
the post *and* the company and may be able to find out more
if you have special queries.

■ Ask those in the know

If you know anyone working at the company, you will get an
insider's view. You can also ask around your network to see,
first, if they know the company or, second, if they know
anyone who knows the company well. They may know the
general field the company works in and the reputation the
company has.

■ Recent news articles

If you are applying to a local company, ask your reference
library if they can help find recent articles in the local press
about it. The internet is another way of tracking down news
stories: doing a search on the name of the company can
bring up all sorts of items from recent stock market
flotations to charity events, all adding to your overall picture.

Other groundwork—the tools of the trade

Although you do not need much material equipment to produce a good application, there are a few things which it is worth buying to help you present yourself in the best possible light to a recruitment manager. See Part B, page 112, for a breakdown of what you should invest in.

See Part B, page 112.

Handwritten applications

How good is your handwriting? Be honest. There was a period when many large companies used graphologists—handwriting experts—to try and work out the character of applicants. The practice is rare in the UK now, but if your handwriting is messy or illegible, the recruitment manager will give up trying to decipher the form after a while. Remember that a recruitment manager probably takes 1–3 minutes to read an application: if yours takes longer to read than that it will almost automatically be consigned to the rejection pile.

Practise writing in block capitals: this is a skill and takes time, but the reward is shown by interview invitations.

Arranging access to a PC is valuable. If you or your family don't have one, ask if you can share a friend's, and check out what your local library or job club can offer. Cyber cafes are now available in most towns and offer word-processing as well as internet access, though this is a more expensive option. If you use someone else's PC, save your CV and covering letters on a floppy disc so that you are not dependent on your friend's PC.

When printing out documents to send by surface post, check the quality of the printing and renew cartridges, toner, or ribbons on a regular basis.

3 | The language of the job hunt

An experienced recruitment or personnel manager spends about 60 seconds at most skim reading a CV.

Introduction

The one-minute presentation

Surveys have shown that an experienced recruitment or personnel manager spends about 60 seconds *at most* skim reading a CV to see if it is worthwhile reading the CV fully and considering it seriously. You therefore have one minute to put your case for being the right person for the job to someone you have probably never met before.

Selecting the right words in an engaging style gives the reader an idea of:

■ you as a person: the way you express yourself and the information you have chosen to include speaks volumes;

■ your 'hard' skills: these are measurable skills such as academic qualifications and defined work tasks/experience (for example, reception duties or project management);

■ your 'soft' skills: unquantifiable additional abilities in, for example, communicating with colleagues and customers; creativity and initiative; motivating a team.

The sum total of these three parts—the **Communicate** building block of the application process—enables the recruiter to gain a picture of all of your personality and skills.

This chapter considers these three stages and finally looks at the flip side of the coin: the language employers use in adverts and job descriptions. Discovering and learning the jargon employers use will enable you to spot the hidden messages an employer is giving.

The language of applications

Conveying yourself as a person

What words describe your personality? Try drawing up a list of a dozen words: six of you as a person and six of you as an employee. Consider how you can include this fundamental description of you into your application. You might use the actual words you have chosen or think of phrases in the context of the application which will portray this essential picture of your personality. Here are two examples to show this:

■ If you want to demonstrate your sense of humour you might include 'and I make a great cup of coffee' when giving your statement for being suitable for the post. Make sure, however, that humorous statements are appropriate: the above sentence would not look right in an application for a senior management role in a traditional organization. In this case you would consider if stating that you have a 'good sense of humour' would be more suitable.

Use humour appropriately in an application.

■ If you are interested in management theory and like to keep up to date with the latest developments in this field, you might look at a way of including some of the latest buzz words in your application. The caution in this case is that you use the words in context without appearing to be 'trailing' your reader or showing off to them. You also need to be sure you understand and can talk about the jargon: expect to be quizzed on what it means at interview.

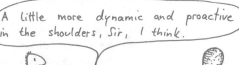

A little more dynamic and proactive in the shoulders, Sir, I think.

The important point to remember when conveying personality is to target it appropriately, From your research on the job and the company, what sort of person do you think they are looking for? You need to tailor the language you use to fit both you and the organization.

Use the right language

Conveying your 'hard' skills

Start to develop your skills in communicating by building up a vocabulary which describes your 'hard' skills and your level of experience/ability in these.

'Hard skills' covers tasks such as computer literacy, specialized skills you need in your current job, and the 'nuts and bolts' type of skills of any job in any career: for example, faxing, filing, and photocopying in the office, preparing vegetables and meat in the restaurant trade, bricklaying and health and safety awareness in the construction trade. Think about different ways of describing a hard skill. For example, if your job currently requires you to deal with people you could describe this as:

- handling queries from members of the public;

- explaining the aims of the charity to people at all levels;

- managing customer service issues;

- resolving consumer complaints.

See Part B, page 113, for an example of a reworded job description.

If you have a job description of your current post, try writing it out again using entirely different words and phrases. Pay particular attention to tasks or descriptions that are exclusive to your company or job. It is easy to use your company's established jargon, and you need to be alive to the fact that someone outside the company might not understand it.

If you have no job description or are not employed at the moment, write down the work skills you have and see if you can create an alternative description of them.

The next step is to convey your level of knowledge or experience you have for each hard skill. For an academic qualification, this is simple as you add the type of qualification (GCSE, A-level, diploma, etc.) and the grade you reached. For work-based hard skills, it can be a little more difficult. You can state how long you have been doing a certain task but it would make a CV boring if you put the exact time length next to each task or achievement. You therefore need to use words carefully to give an accurate picture of your ability to perform a task.

Thinking back to the example above, you might feel that after two years in your current job you are very good at dealing with people. You could therefore add a little more description:

- experienced and skilled in handling queries from members of the public;

- excellent ability in explaining the aims of the charity to people at all levels;

- enjoy managing customer service issues;

- thrive on resolving consumer complaints.

Such descriptions are often where job applicants are tempted to over-exaggerate on a CV or application form. Stating that you are 'fully conversant with PowerPoint' when you have only used it twice is unwise, because you will be found out very quickly. However, vaguer descriptions such as those used in the examples above are accepted phrases in applications. They convey a sense of your ability, experience, and interest but remain indefinite enough not to pin you into making a false claim.

Do!

use a thesaurus to find different words with a similar meaning. You can invest in a book copy or many word-processing software packages contain their own attached thesaurus.

Don't!

fall into the temptation of using long or obscure words to describe a simple activity, or using lots of words to describe an activity or skill that just needs a one word explanation.

Do!

describe how good your skills are.

Don't!

over-exaggerate your skills or use very aggressive marketing language if it is not appropriate to the post you are applying for.

Write it right

How good is your spelling? Check an application form word for word with a dictionary and see how many errors you have made. Keep a list of the words you have misspelt for quick reference for future applications. Expand your list as you complete more forms.

If you are word processing your application, don't rely on the spell checker program as it will miss words correctly spelt but used in the wrong context, for example:

where	were
there	their
would have	would of
wood	would

Conveying your 'soft' skills

'Soft' skills can be summarized as:

- your ability to bring creativity and initiative to a job (for example, do you prefer to be given comprehensive instructions, or an ultimate target which you work out how to get to?);

- the way you manage and motivate people, both colleagues and customers (for example, can you communicate and delegate work to a team, can you build up beneficial customer relations?);

- work preferences (for example, your like, or dislike, of working in a team, having a structured job or preferring a job which is different every day);

- your ambitions and how far you have progressed in achieving them (for example, wanting to make it to the top management level or preferring to be a behind the scenes person who does the support work).

Don't fall into the trap of thinking that every employer is looking for someone who will make it to the boardroom in three years: the people who stop along the way in their career because they have found the right job for their level of skill are very valuable to all companies—and often the hardest to recruit and keep.

Conveying these soft skills can be tricky as they are difficult to quantify and prove. One approach is to set up a list of your soft skills and to look for examples of how you have used these constructively in present or past jobs. Using a solid example of the outcome of using a soft skill is more impressive on a job application than just a bald statement that you claim to have such a skill.

For example, Hannah has included on her list of soft skills that she is creative when it comes to problem solving. Her two back-up examples of using this skill are below.

- Managing a 'problem' employee: no one had previously sat down and actually talked through with her why she was always late for work, rude to colleagues, etc. I took her out for a drink and discovered that she had serious problems at home which meant she was always tired and therefore irritable. I recommended that she took a week's leave to sort out the problems and changed her shift hours. Within six months, she had been made supervisor of another team, and had retrieved the situation with two customers who were considering cancelling large orders.

■ Managing 'problem' customers: whenever we dealt with a certain client, the order always went wrong. I checked the records and discovered that the order was always placed by one person, and always changed by another person for the company. I put in a new procedure for this client, whereby both people had to sign off an order before it was processed by us. Their business with us increased by 20 per cent and there were no further complaints.

Hannah now needs to check which example would be most likely to interest a potential employer and include the relevant one on her application. You can often take your cue of what soft skills a recruiter is looking for from the advert or job description for the post (see Chapter 2, page 19, *Department information* for an example).

Job descriptions and adverts have a further use. Take the words the employer has used in these to describe skills and reuse them in your covering letter, CV, or application form. This shows you have grasped the employer's key words (such as 'comprehensive knowledge', 'enthusiastic self starter') and can apply them to your skills.

Keep it simple!

Some books on CV writing will suggest that the 'best' CVs use the language of the marketing department, for example, dynamic, proactive, motivated, challenging, ambitious. Although this approach may be appropriate for a PR job, for the majority of roles below senior management level, they can often be counter-productive. If you describe yourself as 'an ambitious and motivated individual with a real desire to succeed and progress quickly in this role' when you are an 18 year old applying for the post of an office junior, you are less likely to be selected for interview than the applicant who has said they are 'keen to make a start in an office career, building on my work experience at college'.

The language of employers

Just as a recruitment manager can read your CV and pick up on the clues you have given them (whether consciously or unconsciously) the advert for a job or an application pack can give you all sorts of pointers—if you know how to read them.

You need to be aware of the jargon that many recruitment companies and organizations use to describe a job. Read through the adverts on any newspaper's job pages and you will notice that there are certain abbreviations which crop up time and again, such as p/t, OTE, and pro rata. Part B gives a list of the most commonly used abbreviations and what they stand for. There are also a number of phrases such as 'job share', 'fixed contract', and 'flexitime' which are used as recruitment standards. Again, these are included, with their explanations, in Part B.

See Part B, page 114, for a list of abbreviations used in adverts and their explanation.

Apart from the acknowledged jargon that adverts use, the way the advert is written shows the style of the company. On page 35 are two adverts for very similar posts but streets apart in the techniques they are using to attract candidates. Example A shows a conventional advert, Example B a more dynamic method. If you decided to apply for both jobs, you would be justified in taking a more informal and proactive approach in your application to Example B on the evidence of the advert alone. However, neither advert gives very much information and you would need to do more research on both organizations before beginning to write an application that was well-focused and would be interesting to the recruiter.

Keeping a file of adverts which have interesting, different, or useful descriptions of skills and tasks can be helpful in building up your vocabulary. Do not look just for adverts on your chosen area; check out adverts for everything from education to IT and see what language they use too. Many skills and tasks are common to a whole range of jobs. Using a description from a different career sector can often be effective in catching the eye of a recruitment manager who has become bored with standard descriptions, but take care not to give the impression that you have no knowledge of the jargon of your chosen career sector.

Example A

> ### Poetry in Schools Administrator
> ### £10,000–£12,000 p.a.
>
> The Poetry in Schools Project, set up in 1995, supports five poets in residence at various schools in Lancashire, and arranges visits to schools by poets.
>
> An administrator is required to assist the Manager with all aspects of the Project. You will need to be fully IT literate and have experience of working with teachers. Events administration would be advantageous.
>
> Hours Mon–Fri, 9–5 p.m. Some travelling will be necessary. This post is graded as AO Level 2 under the LGO guidelines with 20 days leave and appropriate pension package.

Example B

> ### DO YOU KNOW YOUR HUGHES FROM YOUR HEANEY?
>
> ### Poetry Officer
> ### £10,000–£12,000 p.a.
>
> Poetry North West is seeking a poetry enthusiast to help set up a new poet in residence scheme with local businesses. You'll need to have plenty of energy, arranging and attending meetings with the Project Manager, liaising with poets and helping to publicize the scheme. Obviously you'll be IT literate, thrive on a challenge, and ideally have some press experience.
>
> Interested? If so, send your CV and a covering letter to . . .

4 | CVs

A CV is a description of you and your career to date. It should give its reader an accurate picture of what you can do now and what you are capable of in the future.

Introduction

The literal meaning of curriculum vitae, the full form of the abbreviation CV, is 'run of life'. A CV is a description of you and your career to date. It should give its reader an accurate picture of what you can do now and what you are capable of in the future.

Putting together a good CV involves the **Research** and **Communicate** building blocks. This chapter explains what information should be included on your CV and how to present that information.

The first three sections take you, step by step, through the various parts of a CV:

■ Essential items: the information common to all CVs from office junior to managing director

■ References

■ Adding quality: the additional items you can include depending on your work experience. This section is broken down into groups of information: personal, qualifications, work skills, miscellaneous items, and how to describe multiple posts.

Ideas on the format of your CV are given in the final section of the chapter.

The essential items

Start your CV preparation by gathering together the essential items of information that must be included on all CVs.

- *Full name*: if you have an unusual name consider making it clear whether you are a man or a woman. This is not sexual discrimination but a simple guide for a recruitment manager who may not have come across your name before and would like to know how to address you correctly in any correspondence. You can give this information in two ways, either by adding your title in brackets after your name (e.g. Kashmira Green (Ms) or by adding a new line called Sex (e.g Sex: Female).

- *Contact details*: if you want to have any chance of being asked to come to an interview, make it obvious how a recruitment manager can get hold of you. You should put in your full postal address, your daytime and evening telephone numbers. Where appropriate, include your email address and mobile phone number.

- *Educational and professional qualifications*: you can list your qualifications either in the order in which you took them or with the most recent or highest qualification first. Use the first option if the job for which you are applying gives no particular emphasis in the job description on qualifications; the second option if a qualification is required or if you consider that your qualification will give your application extra punch. For example, if you are applying for a job which mentions in passing that a foreign language would be desirable and you have a degree in that language start your list with it. You do not need to give details of grades (apart from degrees) unless you have taken the exams in the past two years.

- *Interests*: recruitment managers like to read a CV which shows a person who has a life beyond work. The latest buzz word for this is *hinterland*: the need to show more than just the foreground of your career and present yourself as a fully rounded person. Your interests may demonstrate that you have a personal interest in your professional life, for

Quick Tip
If you have an answerphone or voicemail message on any of your phone numbers, make sure that the message gives the right impression to recruitment personnel phoning to invite you to an interview. A message that is amusing to family and friends may not gain you marks in the recruitment stakes.

Quick Tip
Explain briefly any qualifications not widely known and what level they equate to. This is especially important if you have qualifications gained outside the UK.

 Don't!

include school qualifications such as swimming badges unless they are relevant to the post (e.g. working at a fitness centre).

example, if you work in a charity connected with animals, you might list 'pets' or 'natural history' under your interests. Interests can equally be something completely different from your working life, such as socializing with friends, hill-walking or tango dancing. What you should remember is that you may be asked about your interests at interview, so claiming to be very interested in films when you have not been to the cinema for years is dangerous. If you take an active role in your hobbies, for example, doing voluntary work or holding memberships of associations, details of your involvement should be included. Achievements in your interests should also be noted—wins at sports, fundraising, organizing a successful local community petition.

Career history

The description of your career history can be the make or break point of your CV. The information you need to include is:

- your job title

- the company name and address

- the start and end dates of working for the company

- a list of your responsibilities and/or achievements

- why the job ended.

Of these, the list of your responsibilities and achievements is the most important. This list is based on the work you did in Chapter 3 of rewriting your job description. The golden rule is to target this list at the job you are applying for. You may therefore find it most useful to list all the responsibilities you have held in a post on a separate piece of paper and select those which are appropriate. You can add the catch-all phrase 'other relevant duties as required' to your targeted list to show that you do have other tasks. Below is an example of this approach to devising a list, based on Hannah's last job:

Full list of responsibilities	Targeted list for applying for the post of supervisor in a customer service centre
managing a team of 10 staff	include
handling calls from customers	include
writing daily reports for senior managers	include
backing up the computer files on daily basis	not relevant to the post
taking minutes of meetings	not relevant to the post
training new staff	include
appraising staff	include
health and safety staff rep	not relevant to the post

To make your list even more relevant to the job, put the responsibilities in the order in which they most closely match the job description. The job Hannah has applied for stresses training and appraising as key responsibilities, after managing the team, so she would put these at the top of her list, rather than at the bottom.

You should list your current or most recent job first and work backwards to the first job you held.

Developing your career history

At the start of your career, or if you are applying for a non-managerial post, stick to listing your responsibilities in your career history; for a management, supervisory, or other type of senior post, you should give a brief overview of your responsibilities and then list your achievements. For example, here is Joe's career history:

Administrator, Foyle & Camshot solicitors, High Street, Bagley, Bucks (March–May 2002)

(Work experience post: ended when returned to full time education). Responsibilities included:

- opening, logging, and distributing post
- reception and switchboard
- sending faxes, distributing incoming faxes
- checking general email box and forwarding emails to relevant partners' secretaries
- photocopying and filing.

Arrange your responsibilities in the order that they will appeal to the company to which they are applying. If Joe was applying to a company looking for someone with switchboard experience, then this responsibility would need to be at the top of his list.

Kashmira, who wants to move into a management position, needs to take a different approach to relating her career history, as in the following example.

Sept 2000 to present
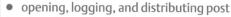
Senior Translator, Andre Gide Translation Agency, 47 East Lane, Manchester M1

Responsible for all translations required by Radio Manchester from English to French and vice versa; managing the French department in the absence of the Director.

Achievements

1. Negotiating the extension of the contract with Radio Manchester for 2 years and the inclusion of drama translations in the contract.
2. Training new recruits in the operational and IT procedures of the agency.

When you are listing achievements, start with what you have managed in bringing in new business or retaining existing business for the organization and move on to any input you have had on the operation of the organization. Kashmira could expand on the example given above, for instance:

> 3. Deputizing for manager when on extended sick leave, including monitoring budgets with the Financial Director: interviewing and recruiting new staff with the Personnel Director.

The additional detail subtly adds to the picture Kashmira is drawing of her skills.

If you have had a break in your career, as Hannah has done, you should cover this in your CV with a one or two line explanation. For example:

> 1998–2002: career break while raising family.

Hannah could expand on this to show that she continued to work during her career break by adding:

> 1998–2002: career break while raising family. Assisted on voluntary basis at local play scheme, as administrator.

If you have had a string of jobs or a change of career so that earlier jobs are not relevant to the role you are currently seeking, you can condense these as follows:

> 1990–1995: various jobs in the construction industry.

If you feel that part of your responsibilities from a previous career phase are relevant to your application, you could add more detail to this condensed version, such as:

> 1990–1995: various jobs in the construction industry, including responsibility for Health & Safety issues.

 Do!

explain briefly any gaps in your career history.

 Don't!

go into great detail for the reason for breaks in a career in a CV but include instead in your covering letter.

Referees and references

At some stage of the job application process, a potential employer will ask you to provide references. References may be taken up prior to interview, or a job offer may be conditional on references. Potential employers will expect you to give the name of your current or last employer and at least one other person, who may be a 'personal' referee. A personal referee may be a friend, or professional connection with whom you have worked—a colleague for example or someone from a different firm with whom you have had close associations.

The decision on which people to give as referees is important. Base your decision on:

- who is willing to give a reference—not everyone likes this task, so make sure you ask your referee first;

- who is easily contactable—employers will want to take up references quickly so a delay while someone is out of the country will not be useful. If you really want to include someone who is difficult to contact, ask if they will provide a written reference addressed to 'whom it may concern' which you can keep, photocopy and send out as required;

- who can give a full picture of your work or personality—not just one particular aspect.

Larger companies may have a policy that only the personnel department may provide references: these are usually short, factual descriptions of your job title, start and end dates, and salary. The most that they will say about your performance is that it was 'satisfactory'. The reason for this is that employment law is now tough on providing poor references which have a detrimental effect on an employee: an employer is more likely to refuse to give a reference than lay themselves open to being sued. If one of your referees will only give this type of reference, look for another referee who will be willing to give more details of your performance.

You will find it a very good practice always to verify your references, sir!

Martin Joseph Routh

You can include the names and contact details of your referees on your CV or cover this item with the short phrase, 'details of referees on request'. If your CV is already long, include referees' details in your covering letter. It is helpful if you indicate on your application whether referees can be contacted prior to interview. The reason for this is you may not want your current employer to know you are looking for another job. Potential employers are sympathetic to this situation and will not disregard your instructions.

Some candidates send copies of written references with their application but unless you are specifically asked to do this, there is no need to do so.

There are a number of errors made by job seekers on giving references. The commonest are:

■ giving out-of-date details, for example the name of a personnel manager who has left the company for which you worked. Before sending off referee details, check that the details are still correct. If you are using a personnel department to give a reference, ask for the name of the person who deals with requests for references.

■ giving incorrect details, for example an old address or a telephone number which is one digit wrong. Again, take the time to check.

■ giving the names of too many referees: if the company you are applying to asks for two names, give two names not four, so that the recruitment manager knows which people you want to be contacted.

■ not explaining your relationship with the referee: make it clear by adding 'current employer', 'past employer', 'personal referee' after the name of the person.

See Chapter 11, Troubleshooting, if you have a problem with providing references.

| # Adding quality: specific information

What information you choose to add to your CV over and above the essential items is up to you. However, the rule remains the same: only include it if it is relevant to the post you are applying for. Think if this extra information will give the CV's reader an extra insight into your skills and character. If you have received a person specification with the information on a vacancy, is there a way you can demonstrate on your CV that you have the 'preferred' items it specifies, in addition to the essential items?

More about you

There are a few other items which you might include in special circumstances to add detail to your personal circumstances, but generally you do not need to include these.

- Your *marital status* may be relevant if you are applying for a job in an organization whose main concern is families, for example, a charity working with family housing issues. Otherwise marital status is no longer a required part of a CV. The same applies to including the number and ages of children: useful for explaining your suitability for a post working with children or teenagers, but otherwise just CV padding.

- *Date of birth*: companies are moving away from using age as a factor in recruitment and legislation backs this move, so it is entirely up to you whether you choose to include it.

- *Web site address*: if you are applying for an IT job which involves designing, maintaining, or writing for web sites, you could include the address of your web site, if you designed and wrote it, to act as a showcase for your skills. Outside this narrow field, it is rare for a recruitment manager to be interested in, or have the time to look at, your web site.

- *Driving licence*: only include this if you have a full, clean driving licence and the post involves travelling.

Some candidates like to include a *personal profile* to give an overview of their personality and skills at the start of their CV.

Recruitment agencies will advise you against it, and for this reason, if you are applying for a job through an agency, you should leave it out. You should also avoid a personal profile if you only have one or two jobs under your belt. Personal profiles are probably best left to senior managers. You will need to spend time writing and honing the paragraph so that it is a useful description of you and your abilities, and does not appear to have been written by someone who has swallowed the latest marketing textbook.

An alternative is to give a list of *key skills* such as 'organizing, liaising, communicating.' A skills list could be useful for applying online (see Chapter 8) where the words can be picked up by a search engine.

More on qualifications

- *Education*: include where you went to school, college, or university if (*a*) you are within three years of studying or (*b*) the company requests 'full educational details'. In both cases, include details of all educational establishments you attended since the age of 11.

- *Current studies*: if you are studying for a qualification other than a degree which is relevant to the post, include details of what you are studying and a current grade (if there is one). If you are studying for something which is not entirely relevant, include this under your interests.

If you are still studying and are applying for posts before your course finishes, make it clear in your CV or covering letter when you will be available for work. Unless you are applying to a company with a graduate or college leaver entry scheme, prepare to be disappointed if you are applying several months in advance of the end of your course: companies are rarely willing to wait more than five weeks for someone to start a job at junior level.

See Part B, page 118, for a version of Kashmira's personal profile.

Always include details of where you studied for higher degrees. You can do this by giving the university name in your qualifications, e.g. MA (Oxon), Ph.D. (Imperial, London).

If your current course of study means you need to take time off from work, you must be honest about this requirement in your CV or covering letter.

More on work skills

Recruitment managers do not assume that candidates are IT literate if computer skills are not included on their CV.

As well as academic qualifications, don't forget to include details about 'untested' skills, which you have learnt on the job.

■ *IT literacy*: an astonishing number of candidates forget to include this on their CV. Check what the job specification requires you to have and list the software programs your experience matches in the same order, for example:

> Fully IT literate, including MS OfficeXP, Lotus Notes, Internet, email packages. Working knowledge of Dreamweaver.

Working knowledge implies a lesser standard of expertise, but an adequate level of competence. If you do have IT qualifications (e.g. CLAIT Plus, European Computer Driving Licence) do remember to include these, drawing attention to software mentioned in the job description.

If you are applying for an IT job, avoid the temptation to clog up your CV by listing reams of programs in their different release versions. Stick to naming those which tie in with the job and group the others under a general term such as 'and various other web design packages'.

■ *Languages*: always put the level of your fluency in a foreign language. Accepted descriptions are: rusty (for those who took an exam more than five years ago); conversational (able to hold a simple conversation); fluent (able to speak, write, and read with reasonable confidence); bilingual (full language skills).

■ *Training courses undertaken at work*: these are courses which have not led to a qualification, but have given you additional knowledge or kept you updated on progress in various fields such as law or best practice in a given area. If you have attended many courses, save space on your CV by a brief explanatory paragraph such as:

> Attended numerous courses and seminars on best practice in customer services and retail law.

List your work skills in the order which they are most likely to be of interest to the company you are applying to.

■ *First aid*: organizations are always keen to have qualified first aiders on their staff so this qualification gives you an extra advantage. Don't forget that first aid certificates expire so do not include this qualification unless your training is up to date.

Miscellaneous items

- *Staff involvement*: such as elected trade union rep, student union rep, health & safety committee member. These roles give a recruitment manager an idea of how interested and involved you become with the company and therefore what you can additionally contribute.

- *Publications*: a list of publishing credits is advantageous in applying for an academic post (in some cases essential) and beneficial in other areas, such as journalism. Outside academic research posts, if your credits are more than a handful, highlight just those relevant to the post, for example:

> Numerous journal articles published, including 'New Developments in Recruitment' (October 2000, *IPD Review*), and 'Internet Interviewing' (March 2001, *IPD Review*).

Handling part time and multiple posts

If you have had a career which has included having a part time job in addition to your full time job, or if you have run several major jobs at the same time, you must make this clear on your CV so as not to leave the reader completely baffled.

For example, Richard once held a full time post, but also had a freelance job. He could explain this on his CV by including the full job in his mainstream career history and adding a new sub-heading 'Other Positions Held'. However, if Richard wanted to emphasize the skills from the secondary role because they fitted the requirements of a post he was applying to, he could include it in his career history as follows:

1980–1983	During this time, I was employed as Office Manager at Allaboutdesign Co. until offered the post above. I was also able to use my free time to act as freelance photographer for Midwest Community Project, travelling to various events and photographing them for the Project's travelling exhibition and publicity material. The Project ended (as planned) in 1983.

Note that Richard has also explained why both jobs ended: an essential factor.

Formatting your CV

Once you have gathered all the information you want to include on your CV, you will need to decide how to arrange it physically on the page. The rules to remember are:

■ make your CV follow a logical **sequence** so that the reader of it does not have to turn back to and fro to work out the chronology of your career.

■ use a **style** that is attractive to the eye and does not bury the essential details in a mass of different font styles and sizes.

Concentrate on sequence and style.

The sequence

Your CV is a story so it needs to have a clear path to it which your reader uses to understand your story. The two basic sequences that are used to achieve this aim are:

Style A

■ Personal details (name, contact details)

■ Education (schools, colleges, university attended)

■ Educational and professional qualifications (exams achieved)

■ Current studies

■ Extra and unqualified skills (languages, IT skills, training courses attended, staff involvement, first aid training)

■ Career history, starting with your most recent job and working backwards to the first job you have had

■ Part time posts, again starting with the most recent and working backwards

■ Interests

■ Referees

Style B

- Personal details

- Personal profile

- Career history

- Part time posts

- Educational and professional qualifications

- Current studies

- Extra and unqualified skills

- Publications

- Interests

- Referees

Style A is best suited for anyone starting a career or below management level. To find the right person for a 'starter' role, where most candidates will have a limited career history, recruitment managers will be interested in educational qualifications, extra and unqualified skills, and career history to assess candidates' potential and experience. For roles which seek someone who has the potential to develop new skills up to management level, achievements in education and in picking up extra and unqualified skills are a good guide for recruitment managers. Aim to use the first page of your CV on qualifications etc. and devote the second page to your career history, followed by interests and referees.

See Part B, pages 120–122, for examples of CVs written in each style.

Style B's sequence is appropriate for more experienced candidates or managerial CVs. Its sequence may not seem as logical as Style A, as the educational qualifications (usually gained earlier in time than the career history) are after the career history. However, this style is all about focusing and targeting. At this level, recruitment managers are more interested in the work experience and skills of a candidate. The educational part of the candidate's life is further away in time and therefore less relevant as a guide to performance and potential.

The style

Most word-processing packages now have a bewildering range of fonts, effects, and layout possibilities. Deciding which to use and restraining the temptation to create eye-catching documents can be difficult.

> ### CV templates
>
> Some word-processing packages now have CV templates on them. Recruitment agencies advise against using these, especially as they are often designed for USA resumés, which are slightly different from a UK CV. You may also find the layout restrictive as it does not enable you to show your personality through the style of the CV, nor your IT skills.

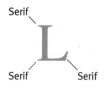

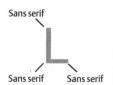

■ *Fonts*: fonts fall into one of two basic types: serif and sans serif. Serif fonts, like Times New Roman, Bookman, and Garamond, have the extra lines at the edge of letters which many people find easier to read. Sans serif fonts, like Arial, Tahoma, and Franklin, have no edges to the letter. The look is sharper and cleaner. Avoid very fancy fonts, for example, those which imitate handwriting or have many curls. Aim to use no more than two different fonts on your CV to avoid 'design confusion'. You could use one font for main headings and another for the text, or use one font for your personal details and the CV heading and the other for the rest of the CV. You can also use effects such as bold, underline, and italic in the headings or to emphasize a phase in your career, for example:

1997–1999 **Travel Consultant**, Maysbury Travel

Use your selected fonts in a size that is easy to read, certainly no smaller than 10 point, and preferably 12 point.

■ *Layout*: stick to the basic principles of making your CV simple to follow and easy to read. Changing the layout every few lines is confusing for the reader.

You can choose to tell your career history in narrative form, with a descriptive paragraph for each job you have had, or you can bullet point your main responsibilities or achievements. Alternatively, a combination of both styles works well for senior and managerial candidates, demonstrating to the reader both your experience/skills and what you are capable of achieving with those experience and skills. For example:

1997–1999   **Senior Travel Consultant**, Maysbury Travel

My job brief was to handle corporate accounts, including managing and training a small team.

Achievements:

- gained two new corporate clients, bringing in £1m extra business for firm
- team won award for best customer service in company

What is the right length?

The standard advice for years has been that a CV should be 2 pages long. If you are just starting out on your career, it can be difficult to fill 2 pages: don't try. Recruitment managers would much rather have a 1 page CV which tells them what they need to know without any extra padding.
If you have a longer career history, it can be a problem to fit everything in to 2 pages. Again; don't try. Sacrificing essential experience and skills for the sake of perfect length is self-defeating. As long as you are sure you have focused your CV properly, it does not matter if it runs onto 3 pages but be certain you are not including details that are irrelevant or could be better covered in an accompanying letter.

5

Covering letters

Introduction

A CV will tell a recruitment manager why you can **do** the job: a covering letter will explain why you **want** the job. A well written, well focused covering letter with a well presented and straightforward CV is a winning combination.

Covering letters come in all styles and lengths, from the simplest note saying 'please find enclosed my CV' to several pages of densely written, persuasive argument. These are the two extremes: a successful covering letter falls somewhere in between.

A CV will tell a recruitment manager why you can do the job: a covering letter will explain why you want the job.

Using and developing the **Communicate** building block is probably even more important when writing your covering letter than it will be when you write your CV. Covering letters show:

■ your competence in written English

■ your ability to select facts and present them in a reasoned argument

■ your understanding of the company and the job for which you are applying.

This chapter concentrates on the selection of facts to include in a covering letter, as many covering letters are spoilt by rambling and irrelevant detail. Finally, advice on structuring your letter is considered.

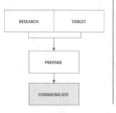

Focusing: what to include and what to leave out

Your covering letter should not be a re-hash of your CV. Instead, you should use it to give depth to the bare bones of the facts of your CV.

Explain your current situation

If you are in work, say what your job is, who the company is and, unless it is a very well known company, explain what it does. For example, Kashmira could write:

> I am currently employed as Senior Translator at André Gide Translation Agency, Manchester's leading translation company. The firm translates radio, television and film and supplies interpreters for conferences and business meetings. It is renowned for the skill and dependability of its translators and its commitment to high standards of customer service. After five years with this company I feel I have progressed as far as possible in my present role and wish to move into a managerial position, building on my experience in negotiating and developing new and existing business, as well as managing staff.

You should spell out your career aims in your covering letter. In the above example, Kashmira has explained why she wants to move on from her present job (lack of career progression is a very valid reason for wanting to move on). She could now expand on why she is applying for the post, as follows:

> The post of Assistant Manager for Foreign Publications, with its emphasis on negotiating and representing the company externally and the department itself at internal meetings, is therefore very interesting, as these are the aspects I enjoy most in my current job.

This demonstrates that Kashmira has grasped the most important points of the job and why they attract her.

Do!

use your covering letter to explain why you want the job and why you would be good at it.

Don't!

make your covering letter a straight re-hash of your CV.

If you are not in work at the moment, explain briefly why this is and, if your last post is relevant to the one you are now applying for, refer to it. Here is what Hannah writes:

Following a career break while my children were young, I wish to return to a full time post using my experience from my last post as Call Centre Supervisor with Macromaster, a company providing out-sourced customer care for a number of High Street retail chains. The post of Customer Care Supervisor as described in your job description seems to be an ideal match with my skills and career aims.

Demonstrating your key skills and experience

You should show why your past and current work experience and skills match the post you are applying for. To do this, read the job description, pick out the skills/experience the company is especially interested in, and show any parallels with other posts you have held. For example, Kashmira has already identified negotiating as a core part of the job she wants and has begun to show that she has experience in this area. She could develop this, as follows:

> As an example of my negotiating skill, during the absence on sick leave of my manager, I conducted negotiations with Radio Manchester for the extension of our contract with them and, picking up on the fact that their in-house drama translator was retiring, arranged for this aspect to be included in the contract as well, bringing in an extra £1,000 per programme for the Agency.

Finding parallels will be especially important if you are changing careers as it will not be obvious at first sight why you are appropriate for the job. In the case of Richard, he could write:

> I feel that my experience and ability to organize a department will be of particular benefit in this post. For example, the job description states that the need to assemble and motivate a team will be vital. In my current post, I have built up an enthusiastic team who consistently meet their targets and often exceed them.

When you are starting out in your career and have little experience to draw on you will need a slightly different approach. You should concentrate on your willingness and ability to train. This means that Joe could write:

> I am interested in this post as it requires the basic skills I have together with the opportunity to develop new ones. I find I learn new skills quickly *[showing the company they will not lose time while you are training]* as, for example, when I worked at the solicitors and was shown how to use the switchboard.

Highlighting additional skills and experience

Look again through the job description and company information to identify less important matches, such as IT skills, educational and professional qualifications, experience in similar roles.

Kashmira has spotted three other areas where there are parallels and writes:

> As required by your job description, I am a graduate in French and German, have first class IT skills including MS Office and Outlook, and am experienced in organizing the workload of my team.

Where you have less experience but can show a genuine *personal interest*, include this in your reasons for being right for the job. For example, Joe has written when applying for a job with a music company:

> I have good IT skills and, as my personal interests include a real enthusiasm for garage music, I have a good grasp of this area of the recording scene.

Joe could add in something about the garage bands he likes to further show his knowledge. If you claim knowledge about a subject always try to give hard evidence of the extent of your knowledge, but don't bluff: you will get spotted very quickly at interview.

 Do!

show you have a personal interest in the main aim of the company.

 Don't!

bluff about the level of your interest and knowledge of a subject.

You need to be realistic about missing skills: not having a good knowledge of a universal IT program will not be accepted, for example, but a skill or experience which is specific to the job or industry to which you are applying is likely to be tolerated, *as long as* you can give some evidence of your willingness to learn, or your capacity for learning.

Missing matches

If you do not have a required skill or experience you can say 'although I do not have previous experience of [*whatever the skill or experience is*] I am keen to learn about this and feel this is not an obstacle to my ability to perform the job'. Add a reason if you can for it not being an obstacle—for example, knowledge of the rest of the job, basic common sense is all that is needed, indirect experience. You should back up this point by demonstrating your speed in learning quickly.

Answering any queries the application requires

Pay particular attention to questions that the advert or appplication description asks you, such as your current salary or when you are available for interview. If you fail to answer a basic question like this, however good the rest of your application is, it will end up in the rejection pile because the one thing you will have given definite proof of is your lack of care over details.

When explaining your salary package, you do not need to go into great detail about side benefits such as pension arrangements. A simple explanation as given below will be enough:

> I am currently on £16,000 per annum, with pension and private medical care.

If your salary is very different (£5,000 more or £1,000 less) to that advertised for the post, it is sensible to explain why you expect to receive a larger or smaller amount. Looking for a larger salary is obviously a good reason to change jobs, but a very big jump from one salary to the next will need to be explained by either (a) the difference between one sector from another, such as salaries in a charity compared to a commercial company or (b) the financial circumstances of a commercial company have meant salaries have not kept pace with the market rate. If you have a pay award pending, you should put this in your description of your current salary. If you are looking at a job that is on a lower salary, you again need to explain this. For example, Richard could say:

> I am currently on a higher salary than that advertised for this post, but because I am changing career, I fully accept that the salary will be lower and the advertised rate is quite acceptable.

What would not be a good idea is to add, 'I would be willing to accept this *initial* rate.' An assumption that additional salary will be forthcoming will not be popular with a recruitment manager.

Do!

explain any large differences between your current salary and that advertised with the post you are applying for.

Don't!

expect that the company will increase an advertised salary amount to recruit you. Salary negotiations are only possible where no salary is advertised.

You should end your covering letter with any personal circumstances which affect your ability to attend interview or when you can start the job. This includes:

■ any holidays you might have booked: use your common sense and defer applying for jobs in the fortnight running up to a holiday unless you are ready to return at short notice and can give easy contact details.

■ any assistance you might need if you have a disability: for example, help with stairs; a sign language interpreter at interview.

■ if applying for a part time post where the hours are flexible to suit the postholder, which hours/days you are available.

■ your current notice period. If you are not currently in employment, state when you can start work.

■ if you are living in a different part of the country (or another country completely) to where the job is located, explain why you are interested *and able* to move. Bear in mind that if there is no relocation package mentioned in the job details, you should not expect a company to offer financial assistance for moves.

Quick Tip
If you have a long notice period check if it can be reduced. Being able to cut the notice period can give you a very real edge. Ask colleagues what company policy is, but be careful who you ask if you do not want your employer to know you are job hunting.

Keeping the best

You should not use the same covering letter for every application as the focus will shift, but do keep a copy of all your letters and reuse paragraphs which are appropriate, to save yourself time.

Keep a log of covering letters which gained you an interview and keep developing these as you are evidently on the right track.

Checking

When you have written your letter and if you have time, print it out and put it aside for an hour or two. You often see places where you can improve and clarify a letter if you return to it with a fresh mind, as well as spotting spelling mistakes.

What not to include

You need to teach yourself the discipline not to ramble in your covering letter. Keep to the topics described above and avoid the following.

DON'T

■ repeat word for word what is on your CV. Simply draw attention to your CV by saying, 'as stated on my CV, I have experience in . . .'

■ go into lengthy detail of what you did to get your educational or professional qualifications unless it has a real relevance to the job. For example, do not describe how you researched an undergraduate or postgraduate thesis and the conclusions you reached, unless you are applying for a job which is all about your thesis.

■ explain in minute detail what you do in your current or last job.

■ write tirades against your current or last employer. No matter how badly a job is going, recruitment managers will not be keen to take on someone who shows little loyalty to the company: such people are immediately marked as troublemakers and will end up in the rejection pile.

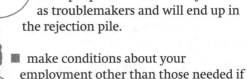

■ make conditions about your employment other than those needed if you have a disability. Starting an application by stating that you are unable to work Fridays or before 10 a.m. is a non-starter, unless this is an application for a part time or flexible time post.

How to present yourself: the format of your letter

Your covering letter should be no more than one side of A4 at the start of your career, expanding to two sides as you progress. Like your CV, your covering letter needs to follow a logical sequence. The following format is an accepted standard:

See Part B, pages 123–9, for examples of different covering letters.

■ *what job you are applying for and any job reference.* Larger companies may have several vacancies and you need to make it clear for which you are applying. Recruitment managers are always keen to know how well an advert has performed and review if any changes need to be made to where they advertise to attract the right candidates. You are the ultimate beneficiary of this process of review as you will hear of more jobs, so take the time to give this information.

■ *what you are doing at the moment and why you want to change this*: your current job and your career aims

■ *what makes you right for this job*: the skills and experience you have which match

■ if requested, *salary details, when you are available for interviews* or *to start work*

■ *special personal circumstances*: as described on page 57.

Use a font and type size that is easy to read: using the same font and size as your CV makes good design sense.

See page 50 for information about fonts and design styles.

You can choose to write in paragraphs or use bullet points to list your skills or experience, for example:

> I feel my most relevant skills are:
>
> - verbal and written communications
> - self-organization and time management
> - commitment to the company
> - speed and competency in learning new skills.

Finally, do not forget to sign your letter.

6

Job application forms

Recruitment managers have thought long and hard to design a job application form.

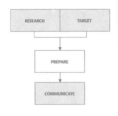

Introduction

When you have written the perfect CV and the perfect covering letter, having to complete a job application form can seem a waste of time. Too many job applicants fall at the first hurdle by deciding their CV and covering letter are more useful and send these instead of the form. But recruitment managers have thought long and hard to design a job application form which will provide them with all the information to make an assessment of your ability to do the job.

Recruitment managers who expect many candidates for a post rely on application forms to enable them to compare candidates objectively. Candidates answer questions appropriate to the post, so it is easy for the recruitment manager to determine if a candidate has the essential skills and experience.

You will need to use your **Research, Target**, and **Communicate** blocks to complete an application form. This chapter looks at:

■ key rules for filling in application forms

■ the core question of any form: why you want the job. Your answer can win or lose you an interview

■ other questions which you may not always encounter but need to know what they mean

■ technical issues on form completion

■ common errors.

Key rules

There are really only two key rules to filling in an application form successfully:

- read the question! The **Research** stage.

- answer the question! The **Target** and **Communicate** stage.

As obvious as these rules sound, a great many candidates fail to follow them.

Read the form the whole way through first and then give yourself a few minutes to think about what is being asked and how you can present the facts required to present yourself in the best way. It is very enticing to rush into filling in a form straight away, but if you do that you invariably find that half way through answering a question you have either run out of space or have too much blank space left.

Be guided by the space element on a form. If the form gives four lines to enter all your education details, you can assume that qualifications are not especially important to the company. If the form gives limited space to describe your job responsibilities, pick those most relevant to the job you are applying for. Alternatively, group responsibilities together under a single heading (such as 'administrative duties' or 'financial administration') and explain in more detail in the space given for describing why you are suitable for the job.

Educational qualifications

Where there is insufficient room on a form to list all your qualifications, select the ones most relevant to the post to give in detail and summarize the rest. Most employers will look favourably on candidates with English and Mathematics qualifications, so you could write 'Seven GCSEs including Maths, English Language, and English Literature.' Higher qualifications, from A-levels onwards, should always be given in full.

Core question: why do you want the job?

 Do!

always take the time to write a proper response to this question: never just write 'I've read the job description and I have all the skills.' You must show some enthusiasm for the job or you are wasting energy.

'Why do you want the job?' is an inevitable question on an application form though it may be given under other descriptions: reasons for this application, supporting statement, or suitability for this position are alternatives. This is the key question on any application form and the one you need to think about most carefully.

Read how the question is phrased to give you an idea of how you should tackle your answer. Some questions will be amplified by saying, 'Give reasons for your suitability for this position, drawing on your experience and skills.' Suppose that

Job description	Hannah's matches
fully understand the product policy for which cover is provided by the team	know the products: this company was one of our big rivals in my last post
supervise team of 4 call centre operatives	supervised team of 6 in last job
monitor performance of operatives	did this in the last post
complete daily reports to management team	this was done electronically in my last post, but did give verbal monthly report

 Don't!

include wanting a better salary or other benefits as a reason for applying for the job. The only benefit that is acceptable is flexitime or moving to part time work if your personal circumstances demand a change in your work pattern.

Hannah is applying for the post of call centre supervisor. First, she would need to look at the job description which came with the application form and spot the matches with her own career.

Hannah could now write in her supporting statement:

Having read the job description, I consider I have the right skills for this post as I have sound experience of similar products to those sold by the company (as you can see from my career history, my last post was with Macromaster, which provided customer care for this range of cookers). I am used to supervising a small team, including their motivation, monitoring, and training. Macromaster had an electronic reporting system which I checked on a daily basis and discussed monthly with the Sales Management team.

More senior posts may require a different emphasis in your answer, as the reasons for your application may be expanded by asking

- what you would bring to the company

- how you would approach the key tasks of the job

- how the job fits in with your career aims.

In this case you need to read not only the job description but also the person specification and find out as much as you can about the organization you are applying to. If Richard has spotted a senior post with a charity he could write:

I am very interested in this post due to its synergy with my experience, skills, career aims, and personal interests. As an experienced manager, used to creating, managing, and motivating teams, the challenge of setting up a new team is both exciting and well within my capabilities. My aim would be to form a team of people who would work well together, be able to meet deadlines and budgets by being aware of each other's work, and who adopt a hands-on approach. I understand that design and production has been a weak area in the charity, and I would aim to reverse this perception completely; building up the reputation of the department through promptness and reliability, so that it became a key and respected part of the organization.

When writing your supporting statement, again be guided by the space allowed on the form. For junior posts, keep to the space allowed, while in senior management posts, write no more than one extra side of A4. Recruitment managers will be looking for a focused presentation.

Supporting statements are the one area on an application form where your personality can be reflected. By writing your statement carefully, you can let your commitment to standards, understanding of business issues, personal aims, or interests be shown in the language you use and the way you present yourself. Using humour (wisely) and enthusiasm can go a long way when you are starting out on your career and have less solid experience and skills to back up your application.

 Do!

when applying to a charitable organization demonstrate that your personal interests match the aims of the charity.

 Don't!

spend too much time philosophising over the direction of the charity—unless you are applying to be chief executive.

Quick Tip
Although supporting statement questions are often accompanied by the phrase 'continue on a separate sheet if necessary' you should not take this as a licence to write screeds.

Additional questions

There are some questions you may not have encountered previously, such as:

■ *Are you related to anyone in the organization?* Certain organizations need to be very clear on possible accusations of bias when hiring new staff. Housing associations, government departments, some charitable organizations, and financial establishments will want to know if you have any family connections with the firm. Such connections will not rule you out of the running for the job, but must always be declared.

■ *Do you have a conviction recorded against you?* If you have a criminal conviction which has not expired, you are obliged by law to declare this. The Rehabilitation of Offenders Act 1974 allows certain convictions to be counted as 'spent' after a given length of time. If you are in any doubt about whether your conviction is spent or expired, talk to your probation officer. Again, a criminal conviction will not necessarily mean the automatic refusal of your application: it will depend on the type of conviction and the nature of the job you are applying for.

If the question is phrased as 'how many days absence have you had?' this does not include paid, booked holiday leave.

■ *How many days have you had off sick in the past twelve months?* Organizations advertising senior posts or roles which are crucial for the smooth running of the organization need to know that potential employees have a good track record on absence, to be confident that the company can be run efficiently. If you have had a poor year of absence due to special circumstances, such as going into hospital for an operation, add an explanatory note and give your usual number of days off sick. Organizations may also require you to complete a full health questionnaire, usually when medical benefits are included in the pay package.

If you need a work permit, state this on the application form, even if there is no specific question relating to this.

■ *Please state your National Insurance number:* employers are required by law to check that potential employees have the right to work in the United Kingdom. The possession of a National Insurance number is one easy way to check eligibility.

Each organization will have its own approach to finding out from you what skills you have. This may take the form of asking you to tick boxes beside a list of IT software programs (often also asking you to describe your skill level) or giving you an open space to list your skills. If the form takes the latter option, select the skills which are relevant to the post, not every single skill you possess.

6 Job application forms

See Part B, page 129, for an example of a skills list.

Equal opportunities

A company which states that it is 'an equal opportunities employer' means it has a proactive attitude towards equal opportunities, and tries to ensure that its staff reflect the population in which it is located and the clients with whom it deals. Its offices will be fully accessible to anyone with a disability. Companies which are 'striving to be an equal opportunities employer' may have difficulty in reaching these aims, perhaps due to its office accommodation or failing to get applications from people from ethnic minority backgrounds.

Do take the time to fill in equal opportunities questionnaires sent out with application forms: it is from these that a recruitment manager can identify whether its advertising campaign is reaching a wide range of possible candidates.

Keeping a record

It is very useful to take a photocopy of your completed application form. There are two reasons for this suggestion:

- if you are invited to an interview, reread your application form and check what you wrote as part of your pre-interview preparation. Without a copy, you can end up at interview trying to remember what you wrote and wondering if what you are saying ties in with it.

See Chapter 9, pages 83–5, for more on preparing for interviews.

- if you write a particularly good supporting statement use this as the basis of supporting statements for other application forms. No supporting statement will be quite the same for different applications, if you stick to the **TARGET** rule, but you can reuse phrases and sentences to save time and energy.

Technical issues

Use the following guidelines to help your application.

■ Always write in black ink. Application forms are usually photocopied and black photocopies best.

■ You will generally be asked to write in block capitals on a form: take the time to practise this form of writing until it is clearly legible. If you have real difficulty with your handwriting, one solution is to complete the form in pencil (lightly) and then overwrite the letters in ink, rubbing out the pencil afterwards. Even block capitals handwriting says a lot about you to a recruitment manager: illegible handwriting will take you straight to the rejection pile, neat and clear handwriting will give you an immediate advantage.

■ If you make a mistake on the form, cross it out neatly or use a proprietary correction fluid. If you make a lot of mistakes, it is worth calling the company to ask for another form and start again from scratch. Any more than six mistakes implies carelessness. If you are prone to making mistakes opt for completing the form in pencil first, then inking it in.

■ You can wordprocess your answers, either if you are a skilled wordprocessor printing them on to the form (but do take a photocopy of the form first to check the spacing is correct) or printing them out on plain paper, then cutting and pasting on to the right place on the application form.

■ Complete the answers to more lengthy questions (such as why you want the job or descriptions of your relevant skills) on another sheet of paper first, then copy the answer on to the form.

■ If you need to use extra sheets of paper to complete your application, always write your name and the post you are applying for at the top of each sheet. Do not staple the sheets to the application form: use a paperclip instead as the staple will only be removed for photocopying.

Common errors

Application forms are deceptive: they look easy to complete and encourage you to be careless. Bear the following in mind and avoid the most common errors.

- *failing to complete the form*: easily done if you complete half the form and then put it aside for a while. Read the form through again before putting it in an envelope.

- *not checking the spelling*: spelling mistakes—especially very simple ones—occur more frequently if you write in block capitals. Again, take the time to read through the form before sending it off.

- *do not use texting language*: write in full English.

- *putting the wrong company name or job title in*: this tends to happen if you wordprocess answers and stick them on to your application form.

No, no, I'm a STRONG team player, not a string player

- *being too literal or too honest in your replies*: Here are a selection of answers demonstrating this point. They were guaranteed to make the recruitment managers involved laugh, but they did not get the applicant an interview.

Mind the spelling

Last employer: Julie, the floor manager

Reason for leaving: I was dismissed

Reason for leaving: Caught my hand in the toaster

Reason for applying: My lecturer gave me the form

If you have had a contretemps with your last employer, see Chapter 11, Troubleshooting, to make the best of the situation.

7 Speculative applications

You need to persuade a company which didn't know it needed you that you are indispensable.

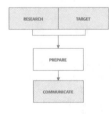

Introduction

Applying for a job you know exists is the easier end of the job hunt. What happens if you can't find the job you want in the adverts but know roughly what you want to do and who you want to work for?

Speculative applications are a test for your communication skills. You need to persuade a company which didn't know it needed you that you are indispensable. Speculative applications combine three of the building blocks of the job hunt: you will need to **Research** your own experience, skills, and interests and the market in which they will be valuable; you will need to **Target** your application precisely, and finally, **Communicate** the results of your research and targeting.

Many people who got their job through a speculative application often say it was a case of their CV hitting the right desk at the right time. This is only half the story: without the preliminary research and targeting, the right desk would never have been found and if you are well-informed of the circumstances of a company, the right time is easier to judge. This chapter considers how to:

■ research and target the job;

■ research and target organizations;

■ target and communicate your application.

Which job?

If you have followed the section on researching yourself in Chapter 2, you should have at least a rough idea of what type of job you want in what sector. However, finding the job that suits you if your knowledge of the sector is only hazy can be a problem. To pinpoint the role that would be ideal for you, try the following routes.

- Look at adverts in the sector and even if the particular job does not appeal, request the application pack. The job, company, and departmental descriptions will help you see what other positions there are. For example, a company structure diagram will show you all the departments and what roles they fulfil. You can then start to target the section within organizations where your career aims and skills are matched.

- Look at the staff and contact lists of company web sites. The more informative web sites will give an overall picture of each person's responsibilities. Note down which jobs most closely match your goals.

- The career sections of newspapers often include interviews with people doing all sorts of jobs in all sorts of disciplines. These interviews frequently give details of how the person originally landed the job. Use their experience to help you both target the job and discover how they got into their role: can you follow a similar path?

- Look at newspaper and internet adverts from recruitment agencies and make a list of those agencies which specialize in the sector you are most interested in.

- Attend careers fairs and seminars where larger employers will be on hand to discuss both recruitment procedures and the range of individual jobs they offer.

Keep a list of the job titles which match your aims so that you can quickly identify these in newspaper and online adverts. You should also keep a list of the jargon used by your sector so that you can use this in your application.

Which company?

Once you have defined the job, you need to research which company is most likely to be open to a speculative application. Here are some suggestions for identifying the right company:

See Part B, page 130, for a checklist.

■ The internet is the easiest and fastest way to research company information. Prepare a standard checklist of information to complete so that you don't forget any vital data.

If you don't have ready access to the internet, consider booking time at your local library or a cyber cafe to do a 'blitz' on a list of names to give you information to work on.

Careers sections of web sites

If the company has a jobs or careers section on its web site, make this your first port of call. These web pages will tell you if the company is interested in receiving applications at the current time and how to apply. Specific jobs will also be advertised. If the careers pages state that the company is not accepting applications for the present, respect this: you are wasting your time if you do not and the company will assume you did not take the trouble to check. You can, however, call the HR department and ask if there is a date in the future when applications will be accepted. Some departments will add you to their list of waiting candidates and advise you by email when they reopen the application process. Otherwise, make a note of the date you are given and try again then.

■ Keep an eye on the financial pages of the newspapers to identify which companies are expanding and what new companies are being set up.

■ Look in trade press publications for stories on organizations in the sector: who is expanding, who is seeking to fill gaps in their staff. Trade press publications often also carry news about staff moves which may indicate an opening for you but you will need to move quickly on these as the publication is probably running some way behind events.

Target and communicate your application

A speculative application should consist of a covering letter and an up-to-date CV, each targeted at the company you are applying to. Your research on the job and the company should enable you to provide this focus. The following indicates what you should include in your covering letter.

Introduce yourself

A recruitment manager needs to know something about you straight away to be encouraged to read on through the rest of your letter. Hannah, writing to a local call centre, has begun her letter as follows:

> I am writing to you to enquire if there are any vacancies within your customer care call centre team. Following a career break while my children were young, I am keen to restart my working life, building on my previous experience as a call centre supervisor.

Explain what you are looking for

This can be covered (as in the example with Hannah above) in the introduction to yourself. However, if you have used a personal profile or stated that you are interested in 'financial' or 'operational' posts, you need to be more specific about what job you are interested in. Richard could write, for example:

> I am interested in managerial posts, ideally connected with design and production issues.

The danger with being too specific about the job role you are interested in is that, if that role does not exist within the company or is already filled, you are writing yourself out of any possibility of a job. The alternative approach is demonstrated by what Joe writes to a music company:

> As an enthusiastic college leaver with a real passion for the music industry and a range of basic office skills, I am interested in any posts where you think my talents would be useful to the company.

 Do!

describe the job you want in broad terms.

 Don't!

be so unspecific that the recruiter wonders what you want.

Do!

focus on the positive
aspects of why you
want to join the
company.

 Don't!

give salary as a
reason for wanting
to join the company:
you could cite part of
the benefits package
(a family friendly
policy), as a reason,
and explain why this
appeals.

Explain why you have selected this company

This helps a recruitment manager to pinpoint what you are
expecting from the company. You might say that the company
is a market leader and you are keen to learn the benchmark
standards of the industry. You could also focus on the company
being new and young in its industry and your interest in being
part of a growing and innovative business.

Demonstrate what you can bring to the company

This is a vital aspect of your letter. This harks back to the need
to show why a company that did not know it needed you will
be convinced that you should join the staff. Highlight your
specific skills (such as communications, IT, similar work
experience) which will be of real benefit to the company.
Hannah writes in her letter:

I believe that several of my skills would be advantageous
to the company:

I know there's an appropriate skill in there somewhere.

- solid experience in a
  similar role

- first class telephone
  communication skills

- a total commitment to customer care
  standards: going the extra mile to achieve
  those standards and so raising the
  reputation of the company

- excellent at motivating a team and giving them
  pride in their work

You do need to spell
out your skills and
not leave it to the
recruitment
manager to pick
their way through
your CV hunting for
skills and experience
which might be
relevant.

Besides the usual concluding remarks of any application letter
(see Chapter 5, page 57) you could finish with one or more of
the following options:

- *offer to work voluntarily* if you are really keen to work for the
  company, or want to know if the job would be all that you
  believe. Larger companies and charities will be open to this
  suggestion: the larger companies because they have the time
  and the staff resources to train and supervise a volunteer,

charities because they are often understaffed. This is a useful approach if you are in the middle of changing careers. For example, Richard could write:

> I have limited experience in charities (several weeks voluntary work) and would be very interested in taking on any voluntary work – whether in or out of the design and production department – to get a thorough grounding in how your own charity operates. Please do not feel that I would only be interested in managerial type work: I am very happy to work as part of a team or solo on any administrative project if this would be of use to the charity.

■ *ask for your details to be kept on file* so that if there are no current vacancies you could be considered in the future. This happens more frequently than you might think.

■ *ask for feedback* on your application, but don't expect always to get a response. Recruitment managers have many calls on their time though they will generally try to give you some pointers.

Who to send your letter to

Find out the name of the person handling recruitment and address your letter to them. Do not send your application to the head of the department you want to join as companies generally have a policy of sending speculative applications straight to the HR or Personnel department.

Do you mean it?

Nothing is more irritating for a recruitment manager to receive an interesting spec letter, only to call the candidate and be put off by lack of enthusiasm or, worse, to be told that the person is no longer looking. Be courteous and inform the recruitment manager you are withdrawing your application for the time being: this can only help your reputation if you want to return to an application in the future.

 Do!

give a broad desired salary range at the end of your letter.

 Don't!

price yourself out of the market: check the going salary rate.

Quick Tip
Recruitment managers are keen to have a 'bank' of potential candidates who they can call on and so avoid advertising costs if possible.

8

Online applications

78% of recruiters said that they would look at an electronic CV before one received by surface post.

Introduction

In March 2002, Reed.co.uk, the internet branch of the recruitment agency Reed carried out a survey of 400 recruiters on online applications. Their findings were that:

- 78% of recruiters said that they would look at an electronic CV before one received by surface post.

- 65% of recruiters are more likely to pick candidates sending electronic CVs for interview than those sending paper CVs.

- two out of five recruiters said 90% of candidates now apply online or by email.

- only 15% of recruiters will not accept electronic applications.

From the recruiters' point of view, candidates who use email or online job sites are immediately viewed as having up-to-date IT skills and IT literacy is becoming more and more of an essential skill for any post.

The message from this survey is clear. Online applications are the way the job market is moving. Candidates and recruitment managers alike favour the speed at which applications can be made and received, the reduction in paper and storage required, and the decrease in postage costs.

This chapter looks at what you need to do to ensure your online application makes full use of this growing area, and how to avoid some of the common pitfalls involved in electronic applications.

Application forms online

The larger commercial companies, recruitment agencies, and HR consultants generally use a combined online application system. This means that you will be asked to complete an on-screen form, and to submit your CV.

Recruitment companies use their online application systems to build up a profile of your core skills and experiences. This profile can then be matched by computer against any suitable vacancies. The form will consist of a number of screens:

Smaller companies will usually ask you just to email your CV with a covering letter. Follow the same rules as for a standard application, but do look at the key rules on page 81 of this chapter to steer clear of common mistakes.

- **basic information**: name, contact details, the type of post you are looking for in which sector, salary

- **skills**: your IT, language and skills specific to your sector or job type

- **key words**: these are what the agency will search on to match you against opportunities it has. Group your skills under headings such as administration, finance, IT. If you find the agency is consistently emailing you details of the wrong type of job, delete your profile and start again.

- **job title**: another way for the agency to search for the right person from its database.

- **work history:** this is usually cut down to the last two posts

- **tests**: see page 77 for more details on these.

- **covering letter**: Don't rush into filling this in. You will get better results if you write down or wordprocess a couple of different paragraphs, before you start looking at web sites. Focus your paragraphs according to the type of job the agency offers. Here are two paragraphs Kashmira has written, one for use on management recruitment sites and another for use on translation vacancy sites, as follows:

> Following a solid grounding as a deputy manager, I am keen to move into a more responsible managerial role in a business which will make use of my languages, ability to lead and develop junior staff and to build up relations with clients.

Quick Tip
Some agencies will specify that you can only use a certain number of words to write your profile so keep a record of the word count for each version of your profile. You could also see how many words you can cut or add to the same profile to give the same effect but with fewer or more words.

As an experienced translator in French with Manchester's leading translation agency, I am now looking for opportunities as a translator with a commercial company.

Both paragraphs accurately describe Kashmira's skills and aims, but their focus is entirely different and will bring different results.

See page 81 for an example of an online application form.

The points to remember when completing an online application are:

- *read the instructions*: the opening screen should tell you what information must be completed; whether you can save part of your application and return to it later if you need to stop mid-way through; the additional documents, such as a CV, which you will be expected to attach.

- allow yourself sufficient *time* to complete the form with as much care as you would a standard postal application.

- *check and revise* your profile on a regular basis. Explore the vacancies on the web site. If you have not been notified of jobs you are interested in, make a list of the key words used in describing these jobs and include them in your profile. Buzz words change quite quickly and you need to keep your profile up to date.

 Do!

read through all the screens containing an online application before starting your application. Prepare additional documents required off-line first.

 Don't!

click the Submit button until you have double-checked each screen.

Web sites will usually give an indication of how long the screens will take to complete.

One problem with online application forms is that their 'one size fits all' may not exactly match your personal career circumstances. If you have taken a sideways move recently, such as filling in time between jobs by temping while looking for something more suitable, this can give your career history an incoherent look. If so, fill in the last two most relevant positions: appropriate skills and experience are of more use to the recruitment consultant than exact career chronology. Your accompanying CV should remain in date order, but explain any unexpected career moves and give prominence to the posts giving suitable work experience.

Online personality tests

Online personality tests are designed to check what roles would suit your personality and career aims best. The tests can consist of:

- descriptions of work and personal scenarios where you are asked to select one from a given a range of actions you could take to resolve problems in the scenarios. The very complex tests may use your answers to the initial scenario to take you forward to a further development in the scenario when you again have a choice to make from a range of answers, and so on.

- a series of statements. You will be asked to select the statement which you most closely agree with, for example:

  - I like to work in a team.

  - I like to work by myself.

The more complicated tests will gradually narrow the difference between the statements and make obvious choices of the 'right' answer more difficult, for example:

  - I value customer service.

  - I value customer retention.

There is no right or wrong answer in any personality test which has been properly designed. They are aimed at finding out your strengths and weaknesses for a role with that company alone. The general rule on these tests is to do them quickly, without giving yourself too much time to think: test results are most accurate if you use your instinct in answering rather than manipulating your answers to what you *think* the company wants to hear.

Online tests can take anything up to an hour and a half to complete. Have a reliable internet connection and allow uninterrupted time to work through the tests.

If you find yourself trying to pick the 'right' answer the chances are you are not applying for the 'right' job: this is a warning sign that if you do get the job, you will have little personal satisfaction in the role.

Funny, I thought I ticked all the right boxes on the application form...

Online or email CVs and covering letters

Your CV is your career visa, your passport to success.

Paul Rapacioli,
www.reed.co.uk

The basic rule for submitting your CV online is the same as for postal applications: focus your CV and letter so that you are applying for the job advertised, not for a universal job that never existed. Here are some extra tips.

■ Most recruitment agencies have tips on writing CVs as part of their web site: take a moment to read these pages and then incorporate the tips in your own CV so that you are sure you are submitting exactly what the agency wants to see.

If it is not clear from the web site which is the appropriate email address, call the company and ask.

■ If you are sending a speculative application, don't send it to the email address of the manager of an individual department: look on the web site for the careers/jobs email address or that of the HR manager. Doing this will prevent your application getting lost in the usual business emails of a manager, or sitting in a redundant mailbox.

 Do!

always use the surname of the person in the salutation of your covering letter (e.g. Dear Miss Leigh, Dear Mr Wedderburn). When addressing a woman whose marital status you don't know, use the catch-all Ms. If you're not sure which sex the person is if they have an unusual first name, call the company and ask!

■ Your covering letter does not need to be sent as a separate document if you are applying by email. The email itself can serve as your covering letter. Write the email as you would write a paper-based covering letter, starting with 'Dear (name of recipient)' and finishing 'Yours sincerely'. An electronic signature is eye-catching but check it can be downloaded easily and quickly.

■ When an advert for a post says just to send a CV, your accompanying email should still make it clear which post you are applying for. For example:

 Don't!

use the first name of the person in your salutation of your covering letter (e.g. Dear Judith, Dear Harry).

> Dear Mrs Varley
>
> Please find attached my CV in application for the post of Fundraising Administrator.
>
> Yours sincerely
>
> JOE SMITH

The pitfalls

The main problem with sending an electronic application is the temptation to send it immediately, without checking the facts of the job or what the company actually does. Recruitment managers can virtually rely on dismissing the first half-dozen CVs they receive by email, because they have been sent by candidates using a 'scatter gun' approach to applications, in the hope that one will stick somewhere. The fact that you got your application in an hour after the advert appeared in the newspaper gives it no weight against the candidate who applied a day or two later with a properly focused application.

The old adage 'more haste, less speed' rings particularly true for electronic applications.

Common pitfalls of electronic applications fall into two categories: **technical** and **style**.

Technical

■ *Sending large attachments as part of your application*: Reed.co.uk's survey found that 48 per cent of recruitment managers said 'that they would automatically bin a CV with fancy video clips or any large, cumbersome attachment'. PCs crash easily when faced with over-large attachments.

■ *Asking the recruitment manager to look at your web site* for all the appropriate information is not a good idea. Why should the recruitment manager bother when there will be other candidates who will have sent all the relevant information with the email?

Use your web site as a supporting tool in your application, not the main resource. For example, you could include your website address on your CV so that an interested recruitment manager can look it up.

■ *Sending an application which contains a virus* is an immediate way of ensuring your application will be rejected. If you have your own PC, invest in decent anti-virus software and use it to run scheduled checks, according to the manufacturer's instructions. Check all attachments for viruses before you send them. If you are using a PC in a library, ask the library how they check for viruses and ask if you can check the documents you want to attach.

✔ Do!

if using a friend's email, work out an arrangement for the friend to pass on reply emails to you promptly.

✘ Don't!

fail to explain on your application that this is not your personal email address.

■ If you are *using someone else's email* to send your application, it is worth explaining this in your email. For example:

> Please note that I am using a friend's email to send this application to you. Replies to this email address will be passed on to me within a couple of hours.

■ *Using a sophisticated design format* within your email, such as text boxes, tables, and bullet points: unless the recruitment manager uses the same software as you, this formatting can get lost in transmission, leaving the recruitment manager with pages of gobbledegook. If you want to make points in your email, stick to typing 1, 2, 3, etc. rather than using the program's function to enter these numbers.

Style

■ *Using an inappropriate format* for your CV: the latest craze by candidates is to send CVs written in Microsoft PowerPoint. This is not suitable for applications. PowerPoint was designed for personal presentations at face-to-face meetings and, harking back to a technical point, PowerPoint documents take too long to download. PowerPoint is not a standard piece of office software, so the recruitment manager may not be able to open the document anyway and that will guarantee a rejection.

■ If you are applying for a design post, you might be asked to supply examples of your work in a variety of formats, but this is the only time that *sending personal promotional documents* (other than your CV) with an application is appropriate.

■ *Taking a jokey, over-informal approach* to the application, such as writing 'Hi!' in the message field of the application. However laid back the company, they will still expect you to take your application seriously, otherwise why should they take you seriously?

■ Make sure your *email address is appropriate*. While zogfromplanettharg@btinternet.com might have amused your friends and family, it will say heaps about you—and not necessarily the right things—to a recruitment manager. Most internet companies will allow you a couple of addresses: keep the joke one for personal emails and have one with your name, or an abbreviation of your name, for business purposes.

The golden rules

■ Focus an electronic application in the same way as a paper application.

■ Take your time: it is too easy to be tempted to send your application before you've focused and checked it.

■ Read through on-screen applications and prepare additional information before starting to complete them.

■ Follow the instructions and tips on website career pages to get your application in the right format.

■ Use your email as your covering letter.

■ Keep attachments short and simple.

9 | Interviews

Assemble and develop a range of interview skills.

Introduction

An interview is an essential part of every company's recruitment procedure. To get a job without an interview is highly unlikely, and you therefore need to assemble and develop a range of interview skills to back up your paper application.

The essential skills of interviewing involve the building blocks of **Prepare** and **Communicate**. You need to be ready to put your case as persuasively in speech as you have done on paper. If you know any recruitment managers, you will often hear them say, 'they sounded great on paper, but were so disappointing at interview'. Don't give up when you get to the interview stage—you are still within the application process.

You should remember that an interview is a two-way process. In a reversal of the situation above, a job that might have sounded great on paper can be disappointing at interview. The recruitment manager must sell you the post as much as you sell yourself.

This chapter looks at:

■ preparing for an interview

■ different types of interview

■ interview questions

■ techniques to show yourself to your best advantage.

Preparing for your interview

There is usually a time lapse between sending in your application for a job and hearing that you have an interview. In that time lapse you may well forget the details of the job description and what you wrote in your application. Your first tasks in preparing for an interview are therefore as follows.

See Part B, page 131, for an interview preparation checklist.

- Reread all the details about the job and the company which were sent to you and make notes of any points you would like clarified at the interview. You should aim to be able to state in a couple of sentences what the company does and what its main aims are.

- Reread your own application and remember what you said were your reasons for applying; the experience and skills you cited as being relevant; any other points you included. It could be very embarrassing to give different reasons and skills at the interview.

Bring your knowledge of the company up to date by checking the company's web site. Look out for new ventures and plans for changes.

Next you need to interview yourself. Practise giving a coherent description of your career from a variety of starting points (from leaving school/college/university, over the past two, five, or ten years), emphasizing the parts which are most relevant to the job. Ask yourself why you want the job and build up an answer from the reasons you gave in your application.

You then need to think about questions that might be asked which are specific to this job. If you have stated that you have relevant skills, you will need to explain how you gained these and demonstrate how you use them at the moment. For example, if Richard has applied for a job which involves dealing with budgets, he would need to be ready to describe any formal or informal training, how he sets and manages a budget, and how he deals with any budgetary problems.

Interviewers will often pose a 'suppose that' type of question, wanting you to solve a standard situation that arises in the job. This could be dealing with a difficult customer, deciding how to prioritize different tasks, working with different types of people, dealing with deadlines. To give your answer the edge, try to think how you could include an example of how you have dealt with similar situations in past or present jobs. An interviewer might ask Kashmira how she would deal with an under-performing member of the team (a favourite management question). Kashmira would need to make some suggestions on how to motivate the employee and preferably refer to an experience with her current team when she has resolved a similar situation.

You should then prepare answers to questions which might be asked about your personal situation. Hannah might be asked how she feels about returning to work after a long break: she could think about constructing an answer showing that she has continued the discipline of work during the break by gaining an additional qualification or helping a friend with work at home. Kashmira might be asked to explain why she wants to move from a job in Manchester to a job in London and needs an answer on how she will cope with relocating and extra living costs.

Finally, you need to think about your interests and hobbies. Informal interviews will often involve finding out more about you as a person, so you should be ready to talk about the things you enjoy doing outside work. For example, Joe needs to be ready to talk about how his football club is doing this season, and which chart releases he thinks are good.

Once you are reasonably confident about your answers, ask a friend or relative to go through some standard questions with you. There are two purposes to this: you will get a chance to give your answers to someone and hear how you sound, while your friend or relative can give you honest feedback.

Technical preparation

There are some 'technical' preparations you should also carry out in good time.

- Check the interview invitation and see if you have been asked to bring anything (CV, example of work). Have it ready by the night before the interview.

- Have a street map ready to take with you: the interviewing company will usually provide directions if you ask, if they do not send a map with the interview details. Work out how long the journey will take—perhaps even doing a dummy run. You should allow at least an extra fifteen minutes for the journey, in case something goes wrong.

- Take the phone number of the company with you so if something does go wrong on the way to the interview, you can ring and explain.

- Check what you are going to wear and don't leave it to the last minute to find your best suit is at the cleaners. You should always dress smartly and formally for a first interview. For a second interview, take your cue from the first time round, but do not drop below the level of 'smart casual'.

 Do!

take a couple of copies of your CV with you, especially if you originally applied on an application form.

 Don't!

thrust your CV on an interviewer; wait to be asked.

Interview nerves

Everyone gets nervous before an interview. There are some things you can do to stop yourself being overwhelmed by nerves.

- Follow the preparation list above.

- Allow yourself enough time to get to the interview and to have five minutes to sit and wait: arriving out of breath and flustered does not help interview nerves and will create a poor first impression.

- Remember that the company would not have asked you to an interview if they didn't think you could do the job.

- Take your time in answering questions. If you are asked something you have not thought about before, it is perfectly acceptable to say, 'That's a tough/interesting/different one. Let me just think about that for a moment.'

- Ignore other interviewees who sit beside you and say, 'I hear they're really tough . . .' Sadly there are some people who like to increase their chances by demoralizing other candidates.

- Smile when you meet your interviewers! Smiling relaxes all your facial muscles, plus it establishes an instant rapport with the interviewing panel.

Different types of interview

All interviews consist of three standard elements:

- **introductions**: you will be introduced to the interviewers by name and perhaps by job title and given a brief description of what they do.

  Experienced interviewers will also 'introduce' you to the job and the company, explaining in more detail any information sent to you as part of the application. Interviewers often use this section of the interview to give you time to settle your nerves: they know that you may not take everything in at this point, but you do need to stay alert and pick up any items that you may want to ask questions about later on (for example, why the current postholder is leaving).

  Your final introduction may be to meet the people you would be working with and to be taken round the office to get a general feel for where you would be working.

- **questions to you**: see the next section for more details.

- **questions from you**: your opportunity to clarify any points which are not made clear during the interview—training and career prospects, the company's plans over the next year to three years, why the previous postholder left or, if this is an entirely new post, the size of the team and its structure.

There are now many different ways for companies to interview candidates from the traditional face-to-face to assessment centres and telephone interviews. If you are faced with a type of interview you have not participated in previously, it really is worth taking time to do some research so that your interview nerves are not increased by wondering what is going to happen next.

Face-to-face interviews

A well-organized company will tell you when you are invited to interview how many people—and who—will be at your interview. Ask for this information if you are not given it automatically: it can be off-putting if you were expecting one interviewer and are suddenly presented with a panel of six. Check out company literature or the web site to put the people you will be meeting in their organizational context. For example, is this the person you will be responsible to, a manager from a different department, or a team member?

Face-to-face interviews can be very formal affairs, perhaps involving facing a board of interviewers on one side of a table with you on the other. In this situation the rule is to try and include everyone in your answers, by looking round at them and not fixing merely on the person in front of you. These interviews are used for more senior posts. Face-to-face interviews may also be quite informal events, with the atmosphere of having a chat with one or more people. Recruitment managers will use this approach when they are looking for someone who will fit into the team or if it is a small company where personality will count as much as skill and experience.

Telephone interviews

Companies may use an initial telephone interview to filter candidates for a post where many applications are expected. Adverts will usually say something along the lines of 'for an initial exploratory conversation, call this number'. Make your call from a quiet, private location where you will not be interrupted and cannot be overheard. Do not make a call on your mobile phone if you are on the move as background noise and possible cut outs will not help your chances. You will probably be asked to give a brief rundown of your career and skills to date and asked a couple of questions on availability and salary. If you are surprised by a company calling to ask if they can talk to you over the phone and it is not a convenient time (if you are in an open plan office, for example), ask if you can call the person back at a given time and arrange to make the call privately.

Assessment centres

Assessment centres may be run by the company which you are applying to, or by an external company which is recruiting for the company. They are used for longer interview sessions,

Quick Tip
Managers from different departments are often used to interview candidates to give a consistent approach in the staff recruited across the company.

lasting at least the whole of one day and often several days. The process at an assessment centre may consist of presentations by the company and different departments, a number of face-to-face interviews, psychometric tests, role plays, and team exercises. Companies use assessment centres to gain an accurate picture of candidates in whom they expect to invest a good deal of training and development. Judging potential is therefore vital and takes longer than a standard interview.

Second interviews

Second interviews are held for two reasons.

■ The first interview filters out most candidates, leaving a short list to be reinterviewed at greater length, perhaps by different managers. This technique is used where managers can only spend a limited amount of time interviewing, so they only want to see candidates who are definitely suitable.

■ Candidates are so closely matched that the interviewers need another conversation with them to make a final decision. Different interviewers may be used, to get a different perspective.

Tests

Many organizations use some form of testing to check out specific skills (IT, spelling, maths), potential for development (psychometric and personality tests, role play, and mock presentations) to filter candidates. The company *should* tell you when inviting you for interview if any tests will be held, but it is worth asking if there will be a test of any kind if this is not mentioned in the invitation.

These tests are not exams so you should not get over-anxious about them; if you do not reach the standard the company is looking for, then the job is not right for you. However, you should prepare in advance to make sure you do yourself justice. Look for tests available to try over the Web, especially those which can be downloaded and kept for future use. There are also plenty of books containing examples of tests to try out at your leisure.

Quick Tip
Filter in this context means to sort through candidates to determine their suitability for the job. It is the stage the recruiter will carry out prior to a full interview.

If you are invited to a second interview, think back to your first interview and consider any hints you picked up about the type of person the company is looking for and skills that seemed especially important. How can you emphasize these?

See Chapter 8, page 77, for more on psychometric and personality tests.

Interview questions

What precise questions you are asked at interview will depend on the job you are applying for. You can roughly guess and prepare for what will be asked by considering what things are likely to crop up under the following headings.

Questions are targeted to the specific job.

About the job

- Why do you want the job?

- What makes you the right person for the job?

- What will be your main contribution to this job?

- How would you start this job?

Break answers to questions of this sort down into sections:

- your personal interest: how the job matches your career intentions and what appeals to you personally about it;

- corresponding experience: the parallels with experience gained from previous and current jobs;

- skills you have already which are needed for the job.

By giving your answer this structure, you can check that you are covering all the points that are important, and give your interviewer a format to follow.

Your basic answer should mirror the reasons for applying you included in your letter of application, and expand on it by referring to points the interviewer has made in their introduction to the job and company.

About your career

- What are you doing at the moment?

- What job did you enjoy most/least and why?

- Why did you leave each job?

■ What are your career plans?

You should be able to answer in one or two sentences each of these questions and make it relevant to the job you are applying for now. For example, if Joe was answering the career plan question he could answer:

> I feel I need to keep all my options open right now as I don't have enough experience in different roles and companies to have a really well planned career, and this is why this job appeals to me, as you are asking for someone to take on a range of tasks—just what I need to give me an idea of all the things I could do and then be able to concentrate on the one that suits me best.

This phase of the interview is also an opportunity for you to fill in any gaps in your career history or explain any changes.

Quick Tip
If you are not in work, give some examples of how you are keeping 'work disciplined' at the interview: working part time, voluntary work, etc.

Ideally, when explaining why you left each post, you should be able to say that you wanted to develop your career, but as this is often not the case, you may need to add some extra explanation. If you lost a job through no fault of your own (such as redundancy) and followed this up with temporary work or a sideways move into a new career, it is fine to say so. For example, Hannah could explain that, although she started out as a secretary in a law firm, her job was made redundant when her firm merged with another. She took on her first customer service role as a stop gap while looking for another legal secretary job, but liked customer service so much she has stayed in it ever since.

If your last job came unstuck, you need to plan the answer to what happened carefully, asking yourself honestly what was the reason. What will be different about this job? Have you resolved the personal problems which caused the upset? Have you sorted out why you had a personality clash with your colleagues or manager? Have you realized that you were just plain bored by the job? If any of these apply to you, you could base your answer round the following example:

> My last job came to an end because I had a lot of personal problems at the time—my wife and I were splitting up and

I'm afraid the job took a very low priority. But I can now confidently say that that is in the past: I've enjoyed the temporary work I've done since then and that has given me the chance to realize this is the job/area I should be in.

About your skills

- Which skills are relevant to this job?

- What extra skills do you have?

- Which skills do you like most?

- Which skills are you missing?

You should target your answer and give a measure of what level you are at with the particular skill. For example:

> I have all the IT skills you require on the job description and I have advanced skills in Dreamweaver and Oracle.

If you don't have a particular skill, show your grasp first of a similar skill and secondly your ability to learn a skill by describing how you learnt something recently. For instance, Richard is asked at interview what skill he has in MS Project. He could reply:

> We didn't use MS Project at my last company, but we used a package which I hear is quite similar—Bloggs Plan. I hadn't used it before I went to the company, but found it very simple to pick up and I found that this type of software back up to a project is very helpful.

About you

- What are your strengths?

- What are your weaknesses?

- Are you ambitious?

- What are your interests?

Your answers to these questions are the stage of the interview when you need to draw on what you have picked up about the job and the company both from your pre-interview research and from the interview so far. If the interviewer is obviously looking for a team player, stress your team skills. Conversely, if you went into interview believing that this was a role for a team player but have realized since then that this is a post requiring someone to work with a team but have their own responsibilities which will not be shared by the rest of the team, you would need to modify your answer.

Questioning is not the mode of conversation amongst gentlemen. It is assuming a superiority.

Samuel Johnson
(1709–1784)

Questions on your personality ('Are you ambitious?') can be traps if you do not think about them carefully. The temptation is to become introspective and ramble, which is not what is required. Your personality in relation to the job and the organization is what is important rather than your personality outside work.

Your interests are a good point for an interviewer to get a real conversation going with you. Be up to date with your interests so if you have listed reading as a favourite hobby, be ready to talk about the book you are reading now and what you enjoyed most over the past year. You should still be a little wary: if you give the impression that you are out clubbing until 3 a.m. every morning, an interviewer will have doubts as to your alertness at work at 9 a.m.

> ## Recording
>
> Keep a log of the interviews you attend, especially if there is to be a second interview. You then have a point of reference to start your preparation from the next time round.
>
> Keep a note of any questions you were asked which you have not come across before and think how you could have answered them differently or better for the future.
>
> See Part B, page 132, for a checklist of issues to log.

Presenting yourself to your best advantage

Interviews are the sum total of a number of things: answers, aptitude and attitude. Interviewers are looking for someone who will be a real benefit to the company. Just as you would not buy an expensive item without careful thought, a company will not want to pay someone a fair proportion of its income without considering all the aspects of that person.

Body language

Sitting up, alert and attentive to the people who are interviewing you, will create a much better impression that if you slump in your seat gazing at the floor. Be aware of the image you are presenting.

Asking questions

Do not feel you have to have a battery of intelligent and fascinating questions to ask. If the interviewer is experienced, most of the points you thought to ask will probably have been covered already. It is fine to say, 'Actually no, because you've answered them all already! But is there anything I've said that gives you some concerns about whether I'm suitable for the job?'

Stating your interest

Do always say at an appropriate point in the interview how much the job interests you. You could say this when you are asked if you have any questions. Expanding on the example above, you could say, 'Actually no, because you've answered them all already! But is there anything I've said that gives you some concerns about whether I'm suitable for the job, because I believe I would really enjoy doing it?'

Stand out from the crowd

Can you find something different or funny to say which will mark you out from other candidates? Interviewing six equally matched graduates at one time, I selected the one who said, 'Yes, I would love this job: please save me from being in the rat race!' His sense of humour was exactly what we needed in the team and he was appointed.

Interviews are the sum total of a number of things: answers, aptitude and attitude.

 Do!

use the same body language you have when talking to a business colleague or friend.

 Don't!

slouch in your seat; gaze at the floor; fiddle with your hair or clothes; stare the interviewer permanently in the eye or look only at the ceiling.

Quick Tip
If your interview was arranged by an agency, always ring and tell them how it went and if there were any unexpected items such as tests or a large interview panel. Agencies do the best they can, but sometimes the company hiring them doesn't tell them what the interview will contain.

10 | Finishing off

Decide if you want the job.

Introduction

This chapter looks at the last vital stage of any job application. There are two parts to this stage: first, you need to discuss and agree the terms and conditions of the job, and secondly, you must decide if you want the job.

The terms and conditions which are attached to a job are the 'nuts and bolts' of employment. They cover salary, holidays, other benefits, and the way in which employees are expected to work, such as hours, policies on training, equal opportunities, disciplinary and grievance procedures. Most terms and conditions are fixed for all employees in the company, but there are items, such as salary, which are areas for negotiation when a job offer is made. Checking out these terms is important as it will give you a better understanding of how the company operates on a practical level and whether the way you like to work will fit in with it.

It may seem strange, after all the work you have put into producing an application that has brought you a job offer, to reach the conclusion that you do not want the job after all. However, you need to take a rational and practical look at what is being offered and determine if it is the right move for you. In the same way that a company is offering to make a level of commitment to you in paying for your skills and experience, training and developing you, you need to judge if you can also commit your time, energy, and loyalty to the company. Making the wrong decision at this final phase can have serious consequences for you and the company, so do not rush into accepting a job before thinking it through.

Terms and conditions of employment

The information on terms and conditions provided by a company with a job description is often brief: details of salary and benefits, working hours, and holidays. More details may be given at interview (and are often the questions you may want to ask about), while an offer letter will spell out in detail these basic terms. Once you start work with a company, a staff handbook or a similar document giving the full details may be issued to you.

When you are thinking over whether or not to accept a job, you need to concentrate on the following terms and conditions:

- salary

- other reward benefits (such as pension schemes, private medical care, bonuses)

- conditions which are relevant because of your personal circumstances (such as flexible working hours to look after children, arrangements for extended leave if you want to study or travel).

Salary

Salary will always be a prime motivating factor for taking a job, but it is not the only factor and you need to decide how important it is to you.

If you perceive the job as one that will help the development of your career, then you may be content to settle for a lower salary.

Quick Tip
Employers are legally obliged to give you a full copy of the terms and conditions of employment within one month of your starting work with them.

Quick Tip
When a salary range is given in a job advert (e.g. 'salary £12,000–£16,000'), unless you can prove to the interviewer that you have extensive knowledge of the job and the organization, you would probably be offered the post at the lower end of the scale.

Negotiating a salary needs experience. Follow the guidelines below.

■ Know your market. Research your industry's benchmark salaries well enough to set a competitive price on your skills and experience, neither underpricing yourself (which may make the recruiter doubt if you understand what is involved in the role) or overpricing yourself out of the running.

■ Sound out whether to negotiate by asking if there is flexibility in the offer when it is made. The organization may stick to its first salary offer, but hold out increased additional benefits. You will then need to decide if these are an interesting alternative, or hold out for your desired salary.

■ Always have a figure in mind when you are negotiating, but be prepared to compromise if you really want the job.

■ Give your own 'salary scale' to the company, saying that you are looking for 'between £22,000 and £25,000', for instance.

■ It is unusual, except at the highest senior management levels, that an organization would consider paying you more than £5,000 above your current salary. Beyond this range, the organization would feel that you are not sufficiently experienced to warrant such a jump from your present salary.

■ Organizations with a fixed salary structure will be less open to negotiation.

Other reward benefits

See Part B, pages 133–6, for a list of the common benefits offered by organizations.

Organizations may offer a range of benefits. Again, there may be some flexibility in choosing which benefits you want to suit your personal circumstances. Ask at interview, or when a job offer is made. Another negotiating point is to find out when you will be entitled to these benefits (most start six to twelve months after the start of employment) and see if you can get them activated earlier.

Conditions for personal circumstances

Consider the other conditions which could have an effect on your personal life. For example, Kashmira's partner, who is a university lecturer, is due to go on sabbatical leave in several years' time and is intending to go to Australia. Kashmira wants to go with him for part of that period and would like more than the standard two to three weeks' allowance of continuous leave. Her negotiating point would be to ask if a six-month unpaid leave of absence is possible. However, she would have to be very careful how she put this, as an employer would be wary of taking on someone who will soon want to be away for a long period. Kashmira would need to accept that a minimum service period would need to have taken place before the company considered allowing her such leave, but she can find out if there are precedents in the company for this happening.

Other personal circumstances are:

- ■ flexible hours to fit in with family responsibilities (picking/dropping children at school, caring for an elderly relative);

- ■ studying: days off for attending courses and taking exams;

- ■ restrictions on holidays: check if you are required to work at certain times of the year, or if holidays can be booked freely;

- ■ assistance with travel: is an interest free loan for the purchase of a season ticket available?

- ■ is there parking space at the company?

We work to become, not to acquire.

Elbert Hubbard

97

Getting the all-round picture

A professional is a man who can do his job when he doesn't feel like it. An amateur is man who can't do his job when he does feel like it.

James Agate (1877–1947), diary

Here is how a management consultant describes how he follows up a job offer:

> One of the things that I have learned about applying for positions is to try and get as many perspectives as possible. After all, if you accept a position, you don't want to find out after the first few weeks that you hate the job. So ask if you can talk with potential work colleagues before accepting an offer. Ask if you can have a look around the office where you would be working. What do you think about the environment? What do you think about the people you may be working with? More importantly, what do they think about the company, the boss, each other? What expectations will be placed on you, not covered in the job brief? Overall, what impression do you gain from these conversations? I have, in the past, decided not to progress with a job application following just such meetings.

This description sums up how you should finish off your job application. You need to be confident that you have selected a post which suits you. Finding out this information is a challenge but you have the following means to obtain it:

■ talking to current employees of the organization, preferably out of the work environment;

■ talking to people who know the organization, especially ex-employees;

■ reading reports in the press about the organization;

■ the general feeling you had at the interview: what did the questions concentrate on? Can you gain a clue from them about what strengths and weaknesses are currently of concern to the organization?

Accepting the job

Always demand a job offer in writing so that there is no mistake about what the job is and the terms and conditions under which you are accepting it. You should also accept the job in writing. Some companies will send you two copies of the offer letter, both of which you sign, retaining one for your records while the other is kept by the company.

Resist the temptation to resign from your current post until your new job is confirmed. Once it is confirmed, resign in writing, stating the day you are leaving.

A final word of warning: once you resign you may be infected by what HR managers call 'gate fever', where you lose interest altogether in your present job. Hard as it may be, fight this off, as you will spoil your last days with your company and it may cast a shadow on future references from the company.

11 | Troubleshooting

Focus your efforts.

At the end of each job application, analyse what you did and where you think you could have improved. Ask a friend or family member to help you —but ask them to take an unbiased view: being friend or family they may try to be too optimistic to be helpful.

Introduction

All careers have a tendency to hit problems somewhere along the line. You may fall out with colleagues, you may be made redundant, you may feel stuck in a rut, you might feel is if your job applications never lead anywhere. This chapter deals with some of the problems that crop up when making a job application.

I apply for plenty of jobs but I never seem to get an interview

Applying for lots of jobs may be the reason why you are not being successful in getting to the interview stage. You need to focus your efforts rather than sending out your CV to every job that looks interesting or which you think you could do. Make a list of all the job adverts which you want to apply to and then prioritize them. Apply for your top five first—that is five days' work. An application should take you a day to write, as you will need to target your CV and covering letter to make it relevant to each job.

Think about the following questions as well. Have you researched yourself and the job properly—are you applying for posts which are not suitable for you? Have you written a CV which is simple to read and focuses on the role? Are you leaving out vital content such as dates and skills? If you are changing career direction, have you explained this? Are you applying for an apparently lower/upper grade post without explaining why? Are you making it easy to be contacted?

If you still get nowhere with applications, start ringing the companies you apply to and ask for feedback. Personnel managers are usually sympathetic to people keen to find work and will give you helpful advice. Listen to and act on their advice.

I've been to plenty of interviews, but these don't turn into job offers

Your interview technique may be letting you down. Ask for feedback from the companies you go to for interviews and be prepared for some home truths. Do not be defensive or offended, but listen to what is said to you and think how you can change your interview style. Ask friends and family to run through a mock interview with you and give you their honest opinion. If you are getting interviews through a recruitment agency, ask the agency for help. You could also look out for interview skills workshops being run by colleges and your local authority: your local library should be able to assist with details of these.

 Do!

work on your interview technique with the help of friends, family, and business colleagues.

 Don't!

take criticism negatively; listen to what is said and try following the suggestions to see what happens.

If you are confident that your technique is right, then you need to think about what you are saying at the interview. Are you, in effect, living up to what you say on your CV? If you claim to be knowledgeable about, for example, budgets and financial matters on your CV, but are unable to answer the interview questions, then you will need to rethink the way you have written your CV and whether you are applying for the right kind of job.

Finally, you need to consider if you are pricing yourself out of your particular job market. If you are consistently asking for more than other candidates, then you are unlikely to obtain a job offer. Recheck the going rate for the job from friends in similar roles and other adverts. Avoid using internet salary surveys, which tend to be aimed at the high end of the scale and can only provide generalized salary advice.

How do I make my CV more interesting?

A bland, cover-all CV is guaranteed to get you nowhere. However, resist the temptation to use a jazzy design (unless you are applying for a design post) to boost your CV, and concentrate on the content. Keep to the rules:

■ make it relevant through research and targeting;

■ make it short, even cutting down to one side of A4.

Use language to liven up your CV without allowing it to ramble away from the point. Using positive, action words to describe your skills, experience, and achievements helps take your CV out of the general run and make it more confident. Examples are: 'first class IT skills', 'four years' solid experience of customer service', 'met and exceeded sales targets', 'enjoy the challenge of a pressured environment', 'like to become actively involved in staff activities'.

Don't forget to use your interests section as a way of interesting the reader. 'Charity parachuting' or 'county tiddly winks champion' will always be more entertaining and attractive to a recruitment manager than 'watching television'.

> **Warning!**
>
> Don't overdo the self-marketing aspect of your CV, unless you are applying for a sales post in a company which has a reputation for being competitive and aggressive. Outside the sales arena, HR managers are more likely to be looking for a team player than a team rival.

I never seem to have the right level of experience for the job

This is a very frustrating situation to be in. When you start out it can seem impossible to find a job, because everyone demands experience, while later on if you want to change direction, employers can be scared off by your being over-qualified. There are two approaches to resolving this situation.

- Turn your lack of experience or over-qualification into an asset in your covering letter. Here's what a management consultant does when faced with the situation:

    I can sell my lack of experience as a strength because I have no preconceptions or prejudices, I can bring fresh ideas, and am eager to learn more.
    I can sell my over-qualified experience as a strength because I bring a wealth of practical experience coupled with pragmatism based on a level of maturity that few others can offer.

    You would still need to explain what may seem to be a retrograde step in your career (e.g. change of tack, getting back to work after a break, looking for a less stressful post).

    You do need to match this approach to the job. A company looking for an office junior will not be tempted by an over-qualified person, nor will an employer looking for a team supervisor be convinced by a college leaver.

- Look for ways to increase your experience through voluntary work, temping, odd jobs for friends and family. Whatever you do will always become useful at some point in your career.

I am worried about the reference I will get from my last company

If you fell out with your last employer, getting a reference can be a concern. However, under employment legislation, an employer providing a poor reference must be able to prove their criticism. A number of legal cases have made many companies reluctant to give a reference if the employee was unsatisfactory but no disciplinary action was taken and the employee left of their own accord. Alternatively, the employer may decide to give a bare, factual reference, merely stating the dates of employment and the job that was held.

How I love a colleague-free day! Then I can really get on with the job.

Hugh Dalton (1887–1962), diary

The other point to remember is that you are not obliged to cite your manager as the person to give a reference: if you worked for a company with an HR department, you can direct reference enquiries to the HR department. This is useful if you

Do!

make sure you have one good reference to rely on.

Don't!

believe the press stories that employers don't check references: they do and if you are caught out giving false information your job will be forfeit.

It's a recession when your neighbour loses his job; it's a depression when you lose yours.

Harry S. Truman
(1884–1972), *Observer*

had a personality clash with your manager but otherwise the job was fine. You could also cite other managers with whom you worked well.

If you were dismissed from your last post you do have a problem. The first thing is to get back into the job market as soon as possible through temping, casual work, and friends and family. You will then have one solid work reference to start building on.

I've had several changes of career direction: how will this affect my chances?

It all depends how you approach it in your CV and covering letter. Do not give too much prominence to past careers other than to emphasize any transferable skills which you can 'carry forward' into your next career. Group together jobs in an industry sector which you have now left behind, as shown in the example in Chapter 4, page 41.

Your covering letter should explain why you have decided to make your new career change and why you think this phase will last: employers will be doubtful about employing someone who only lasts six months in one career.

My questions always sound so dull when an interviewer asks me if I have anything to ask

You should certainly try to avoid 'filler' questions about when the company was established and how many employees there are—these are points that should have been covered in your own research about the organization. You should also avoid asking about salary and benefits until the interviewer raises this question, as you may sound as if you are more interested in the benefits than the job.

Look instead at the larger aspects of the role and the company. If not already covered at interview, ask what the employer wants the role to achieve over the next one to five years, and then move on to where that fits into the company aims for the next one to five years. You could also ask about the culture and 'feel' of the company: what opportunities are there for staff to have a say in policy? How long is the average length of service of staff? Would the interviewer describe the company as structured or informal?

Do not feel that you must ask lots of questions: two to three questions from posts below senior management level are plenty.

Part B: Reference section Contents

Flow chart of the job application process

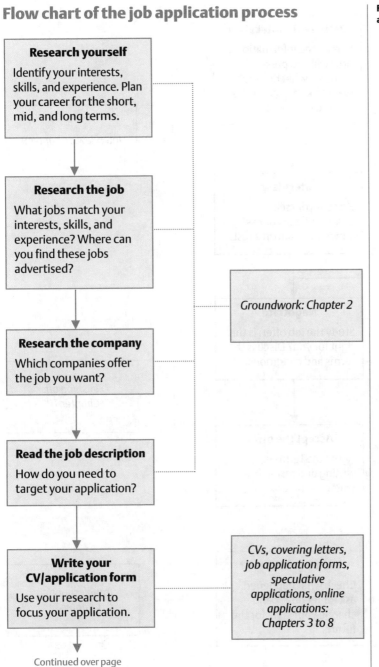

Research yourself

Identify your interests, skills, and experience. Plan your career for the short, mid, and long terms.

Research the job

What jobs match your interests, skills, and experience? Where can you find these jobs advertised?

Groundwork: Chapter 2

Research the company

Which companies offer the job you want?

Read the job description

How do you need to target your application?

Write your CV/application form

Use your research to focus your application.

CVs, covering letters, job application forms, speculative applications, online applications: Chapters 3 to 8

Continued over page

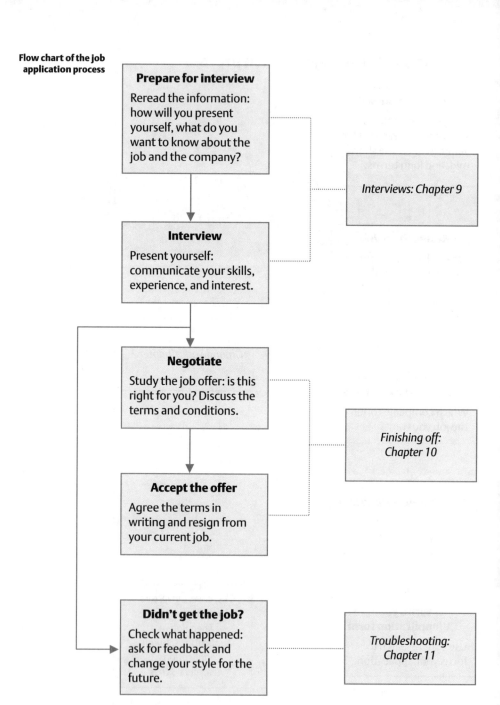

Flow chart of the job application process

Prepare for interview

Reread the information: how will you present yourself, what do you want to know about the job and the company?

Interviews: Chapter 9

Interview

Present yourself: communicate your skills, experience, and interest.

Negotiate

Study the job offer: is this right for you? Discuss the terms and conditions.

Finishing off: Chapter 10

Accept the offer

Agree the terms in writing and resign from your current job.

Didn't get the job?

Check what happened: ask for feedback and change your style for the future.

Troubleshooting: Chapter 11

Researching yourself

See Chapter 2, page 11. Before you start applying for jobs, target what you want to do by working through the following questions.

What are my technical skills (qualifications, IT)? What are my soft skills (communicating, managing, motivating, coordinating)? What experiences have I built up?

What do I like doing outside work? What organizations do I belong to? What non-work activities am I actively involved in?

Interests

Skills and experience

Best and worst aspects of work

Short, mid, and long term aims

What do I like doing most? What do others think I am best at? What do I like least about my job? Is this my weakness or the company's?

What do I want to be doing in six months' time, in one year's time, in three years' time?

Do not forget to get a second opinion from family or friends or colleagues. Ask them to list:

- what they think your skills and experience are

- what your strongest points are

- what your weakest points are.

The greatest thing in the world is to know how to be oneself.

Montaigne, *Essais* (1580)

Example of a job description with notes

See Chapter 2, page 18.   Below is an example of a job description which you might receive with an application pack, with the type of notes you need to make when reading it.

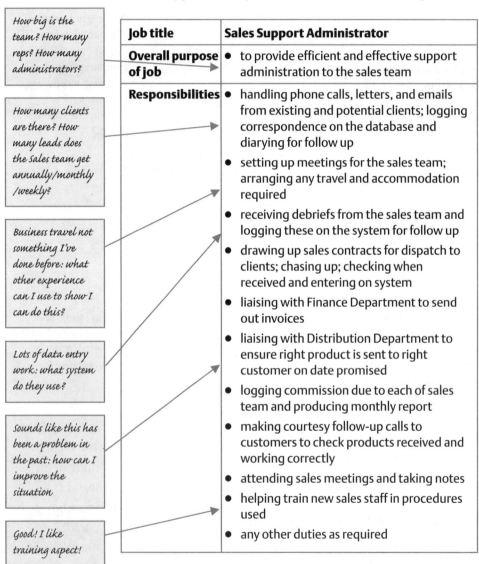

How big is the team? How many reps? How many administrators?

How many clients are there? How many leads does the Sales team get annually/monthly /weekly?

Business travel not something I've done before: what other experience can I use to show I can do this?

Lots of data entry work: what system do they use?

Sounds like this has been a problem in the past: how can I improve the situation

Good! I like training aspect!

Job title	Sales Support Administrator
Overall purpose of job	• to provide efficient and effective support administration to the sales team
Responsibilities	• handling phone calls, letters, and emails from existing and potential clients; logging correspondence on the database and diarying for follow up
	• setting up meetings for the sales team; arranging any travel and accommodation required
	• receiving debriefs from the sales team and logging these on the system for follow up
	• drawing up sales contracts for dispatch to clients; chasing up; checking when received and entering on system
	• liaising with Finance Department to send out invoices
	• liaising with Distribution Department to ensure right product is sent to right customer on date promised
	• logging commission due to each of sales team and producing monthly report
	• making courtesy follow-up calls to customers to check products received and working correctly
	• attending sales meetings and taking notes
	• helping train new sales staff in procedures used
	• any other duties as required

Example of a person specification

See Chapter 2, page 19. In the same way that you make notes about a job description, you should make notes on the person specification that comes with an application pack. Here is the person specification that goes with the job of Sales Support Administrator.

	Essential	Desirable	
Personal Attitude	• Outgoing, friendly • Flexible; able to turn quickly from one task to another • Patient, diplomatic • High standards of accuracy and attention to detail	• Demonstrable experience	*I think I am all of these, and my job at Smith's called for accuracy*
Experience	• Minimum 12 months' work experience • Previous work in customer-orientated environment • Used to working in pressured environment • Team working	• Sales department or customer service experience • Working to deadlines • Liaising with other departments	*Customer service experience (2 years); had to work to deadlines at Smiths, and have done plenty of team working before, bit of liaison with job at MFGplc.*
IT	• Access • Excel • Word, PowerPoint • Email	• Bespoke databases • Sage • MS Outlook	*Yes! All except Sage*
Other skills and qualifications	• Letter writing • Telephone work • A-level English		*Plenty of letter writing at Smiths (and email), not so much phone work. B Grade A-level English*

111

The tools of the trade

Give us the tools and we will finish the job.

Winston Churchill (1874–1965), radio broadcast (1941)

See Chapter 2, page 27. Having the right items to hand will make sure that you don't waste time when you want to apply for a job, and present yourself well.

■ **paper**: White or cream shades are the most acceptable shades of paper: you should certainly avoid papers with a strong colour. This is because applications are usually photocopied for additional copies to be sent to other managers involved in the recruitment process, and deep colours will not photocopy well. Avoid ruled and/or punched paper which does not look professional. 80gsm paper is fine, though you may choose to have a heavier weight for your covering letter.

If you find it difficult to write freehand in straight lines, buy an A4 size blank pad which generally come with a ready ruled sheet to place below each blank sheet: the lines show through the paper. Try to keep to A4 size paper as this makes photocopying much easier and, again, looks more professional.

■ **pen**: Invest in a good pen. Blotchy ball-points will gain you no marks for presentation. Choose a pen that has black ink: black ink photocopies much better than blue. If you prefer to use a fountain pen, discard the one that blots at unexpected moments, and also buy a stock of blotting paper so that application forms are not spoilt by wet ink.

■ **envelopes**: Buy strong envelopes so that your application is not mangled in the post system and does not arrive on the recruitment manager's desk ripped nor with dog-eared corners.

■ **stamps**: It can be useful to check how much your covering letter, CV and envelope cost to send by first class post. Buy in a stock of stamps at the right price, so that you will be able to send out applications without delay.

 Do!

use black ink for printing CVs and writing application forms.

 Don't!

use lots of colours on your CV as it will not photocopy well.

Example of a reworded job description for use on a CV

See Chapter 3, page 30. You should not use the official description of your job on your CV as this will make it bland and dull. Instead, engage your reader by taking the separate tasks and showing your experience, skill, and achievement in each of them. Looking back to the standard job description on page 110, this is how it could be reworded.

Sales Support Administrator

The main aim of this job is to provide top class support administration to the sales team.

- extensive client liaison by phone, letter, and email, leading to building up good client relations with both new and existing customers; acting as their first point of contact to resolve any queries and difficulties
- working with the sales reps to understand their individual ways of working and personalities, thus being able to book meetings with clients with whom they would work well; diplomatically chasing up the reps for debriefs after meetings and encouraging them to follow up on any promises made to clients; ensuring commission claims are sent in promptly and resolving any queries that arise
- using the database constructively, by prompt, accurate, and full data entry, so that a full picture of each client is quickly available; maintaining the diary correctly to ensure client expectations are not disappointed by missed or late events
- liaising with other departments to ensure that the whole sales process from first contact to invoicing maintains the same high standard
- helping new sales staff settle in, training them on products and procedures. Team has increased by four in the past twelve months
- all other administrative duties which assist the team, including maintaining paper files, minuting, producing reports from the system, expense claims.

Note that not every duty on the job description has been used in the CV description: the applicant has read the job description for the new job he is applying for and discarded any duties which are not relevant.

The language of job adverts

See Chapter 3, page 34. Below are explanations of various abbreviations and expressions commonly used in job adverts.

■ **a.a.e.** or **a.e.**: according to age and experience *or* according to experience. Used in conjunction with salary details, for example £12,000–£14,000 a.e., meaning that the salary offered to you would be dependent on previous relevant experience.

■ **application pack**: a pack containing information on an advertised job, usually consisting of a job description, a person specification, information on the organization, recruitment procedures that will be used, terms of employment including salary, benefits, hours of work and holidays.

See Chapter 2, pages 18–20, for more on application packs.

■ **audio**: audio typing: used in secretarial and administrative jobs to show the need to be able to type up dictation tapes.

■ **circa**, as in *salary circa £20,000*: in the region of. The company will be offering a salary around the £20,000 mark. A rule of thumb is that the salary will be somewhere between £1,000 below and £2,000 above the stated figure.

■ **covering letter**: a letter to be sent with a CV or application form, setting out in detail why you are applying for the job.

■ **FAO**: For the Attention Of in the context of 'mark your application FAO Fiona Smith, HR Department'.

■ **f/t** or **F/T**: full time. Jobs are classed as 'full time' which require you to work for five days, totalling between 35 hours and 40 hours per week.

The Employment Act 2002 has given fixed term workers the same rights as permanent staff, so make sure of the benefits package when accepting a fixed term post. However, be prepared to be flexible: fixed term workers may be paid at a higher rate to compensate them for benefits such as pensions, so that they can set these types of schemes up for themselves.

■ **fixed term**: These are jobs which have a definite ending date, rather than a permanent job which has no end date and theoretically could run until the employee retires. Fixed term contract jobs are often involved with projects which run for a predetermined length of time. Fixed term contracts may also be used by companies when they are not sure if they can afford to pay for another permanent member of staff, but want to test out how beneficial the job (and the jobholder) are to the company. If your job falls into the latter category, you need continuously to prove yourself indispensable so that the post becomes permanent.

■ **flexitime**: Flexitime covers a system of working whereby you undertake to work for a given number of hours a week or month, but determine what time you start and finish each day. You may be required to be present for **core hours**, such as 10 a.m. to 3 p.m., when the office expects to be at its busiest. Flexitime may also mean that there is no overtime: if you do more hours than required, you take time off in lieu of payment. Check which flexitime system the employer operates, and especially what are the core hours, if you have personal commitments at certain times of the day.

■ **hinterland**: Your personal interests and hobbies are your 'hinterland' on a CV or job application, providing the recruiter with an opportunity to perceive you as a fully rounded person, with a life outside work.

■ **hpw**: hours per week. Used in the sense '35 hpw, Mondays to Fridays.'

■ **HR**: Human Resources. This is the modern term for Personnel, and means rather more. Personnel tends to be the basics of employment such as salaries and terms and conditions. HR looks beyond the small details to understanding that people are a company's most important and valuable asset, and planning how to use this 'resource' to the company's best benefit. HR is involved with whole strategies, building in every part of an organization's needs and aims.

■ **job share**: A fairly recent innovation, job sharing means the sharing of a single job between two or more people who work at different times. It is very popular with employees who wish to spend more time with their family, or have other personal interests to pursue. To job share successfully, you need:

● to know your job partner well and get on with them;

● to be able to communicate with each other to a very high standard;

Nothing is really work unless you would rather be doing something else.

J. M. Barrie

- to work in the same style, as you must be able to pick up exactly where the other person left off.

Job sharing used to be confined to higher management and professional posts, such as solicitors. However, job sharing is now becoming more frequent at every level. If you have a friend who would you like to job share with, it is worth writing joint applications to see if an employer is interested.

■ **k**: thousand, so £18k = £18,000.

■ **LW** or **LWA**: London Weighting or London Weighting Allowance. Because of the higher costs of living, an additional amount may be paid by companies operating across the UK or other organizations (such as the emergency services) which have a national pay structure. Outer and Inner London weighting may also be paid, reflecting the fact that costs get progressively higher the closer in to London you work. Note that you do not have to be living in London to qualify for this extra amount: it is the job which attracts the weighting.

■ **no agencies**: The company advertising the job will not accept applications sent by recruitment agencies, as the company does not wish to pay agency fees. Useful to know if you are registered with one or more agencies as your CV will definitely not have been sent to the advertiser.

■ **OTE**: On Target Earnings. Sales and promotional jobs often have quite a small basic salary while the rest is made up of commission. The OTE figure tells you more than how much you might make if you are good at the job, it is also the amount the company *expects* you to make. Check carefully how the commission is calculated to give you an idea of how much business you must do, and decide if you are capable of handling the work and pressure involved in reaching that target.

■ **p.a.**: per annum, literally 'for the year'. Used in conjunction with a salary to show the amount you will be paid in each calendar year, for example £14,000 p.a.

■ **PA**: Personal Assistant. A senior administrative job, usually providing support to one person or a small team. Often

Work is what you do so that some time you won't have to do it any more.

Alfred Polgar

described as being the 'right-hand person' type of role, to show the depth of reliance placed on the jobholder.

■ **PR**: Public Relations. PR is the presentation of a company to the outside world and generally refers to relations with clients and the press. However, the organization may also include marketing, communicating with internal departments, and any other form of contact with staff and clients under this catch-all title.

■ **PRP**: Performance Related Pay. PRP ties in salary to the individual employee's performance and/or the performance of the team, department, or company as a whole over a set period. Employees are paid a basic salary, and then a bonus depending on whether targets are met in full or in part. PRP structures can be very rewarding for hard work, but can also be complicated with many built-in provisos, so ensure that you understand the scheme before signing up to it.

■ **pro rata**: literally 'according to the rate'. Used in conjunction with salary where the job is part time or for a fixed term of less than a calendar year. The salary will be given as, for example, '£20,000 per annum pro rata.' This means that if you were doing the job full time, or for a full year, the salary would be £20,000, but it will be reduced proportionally by the hours or length of your job. Thus if you worked four days, the salary would be reduced by a fifth to £16,000 or if your job lasts for six months, you would be paid a total of £10,000 in that time.

■ **p/t** or **P/T**: part time. Where a job is for less hours or days than the organization's standard hours or days, it is part time. The job still counts as being permanent.

■ **s/h**: shorthand. It is applied to secretarial posts which require the jobholder to be able to take shorthand dictation.

■ **SME**: Small and Medium Enterprises; refers to business organizations with less than 500 staff. There are now a considerable number of jobs in the market which deal with the promotion of or giving assistance to SMEs, as part of local or national business initiatives. You will need to have a good grasp

Quick Tip
The salary quoted in adverts is almost always gross, before the deduction of tax and insurance contributions. Take this into account when calculating what salary you need to cover living expenses.

Recent legislation has ensured part time workers must have access to the same benefits as full time workers.

of the issues faced by SMEs, preferably from first hand
experience, if you are attracted by such roles.

- **working knowledge**: This means your knowledge of a skill
(for example, of a software program) should be sufficient for
you to use it easily in a job, though you may not have had
formal training in it.

- **WPM**: Words Per Minute. Used in relation to the speed at which
you must be able to type (60 wpm) or at which you can take
shorthand dictation (100 wpm). To see how fast you are, type a
page or pages from a book for exactly five minutes onto a
wordprocessor. Then count the words you have typed (most
word-processing packages can do this for you) and divide by five
to get your minute rate. To check shorthand speed, use the
same passage you have typed and ask a friend or relative to read
it out while you take it down in shorthand, again for five
minutes. Your rate will be slightly faster as you already know
the passage, so deduct 10 per cent from your final figure.

Kashmira's personal profile

See Chapter 4, page 45. Kashmira has decided to add a
personal profile to her CV. To get started, she jots down key
words she could use to describe herself and her skills to date:

Languages	Well organized
Managing department while manager away	
Motivated	Loyal to company
Good with clients	Negotiating
Dealing with that awkward administrator!	
Trained new staff	

From this, Kashmira constructs her first draft, as follows:

> Skilled translator in idiomatic French and German, with a particular fluency in 19th-century literature. Previous management experience while manager on sick leave.

The problem with this is that, as an aid to helping Kashmira towards a management post, it says very little about her potential as a management candidate and, with the emphasis on the languages side, it precludes her from jobs not wholly dedicated to translation. An alternative version might read:

> Well organized and motivated individual, with experience in managing a small department and keen to move forward into a permanent management post. Knowledge of budgets, personnel matters, and used to training and delegation of tasks.

This is a better profile, demonstrating Kashmira's existing experience and eagerness to develop but it still needs improving. At the moment 90 per cent of management candidates could probably write the same paragraph. Kashmira would need to find the extra individualistic edge that would make her profile different from the rest.

> Languages graduate and enthusiast with well-honed skills in the management of a small department including personnel, training and budgetary matters. Proven successful negotiating skills, within and outside the company. High standards of self-organization and motivation, keen to make a contribution to a company in return for the opportunity to develop management skills.

 Do!

aim for your personal profile to be somewhere around 50 to 100 words.

 Don't!

include your personal profile on your CV when sending to an agency.

The above example strikes the right balance between demonstrating Kashmira's individual talents (language), alongside her success to date in management. It also shows what Kashmira is looking for from a prospective employer, and what they can expect from her.

Examples of CVs

CV Style A

See Chapter 4,
pages 48–49.

PERSONAL DETAILS

Name: **Joe Smith**
Address: 47 Brook Street, Southampton SO2 1NN
Telephone: (home) 0231234567 (mobile) 07950 124657
Date of
Birth: 18 October 1984

EDUCATION

1995–2000   Southampton Priory School
2000–2002   Southampton College

QUALIFICATIONS

1995   GCSEs: Maths (B), English Language (B), English
            Literature (C), Computer Studies (A), CDM (B), French
            (C), Spanish (C), Science (B)
2002   BTECH

As Joe has just finished this course, he could put in more details if the course was relevant to the job he was applying for.

ADDITIONAL SKILLS

IT   MS Office including Excel and Access; email; internet
First aider St John's Ambulance, 2002

WORK EXPERIENCE

March–May   **Administrator**, Foyle & Camshot solicitors, High
2002   Street, Bagley, Bucks
            (*Work experience post: ended when returned to full time
            education*). Responsibilities included:
- opening, logging, and distributing post
- reception and switchboard
- sending faxes; distributing incoming faxes
- checking general email box and forwarding emails
  to relevant partners' secretaries
- photocopying and filing.

Always put in the date of employment

INTERESTS

Music (garage, blues); football (support
Southampton), first aid—joined St John's Ambulance
Brigade, summer 2002

REFERENCES available on request

CV Style B

See Chapter 4, pages 48-9.

RICHARD JOHN JONES
The Maples, Rhosnesni, Herefordshire HR26 2ZZ
Tel (h) 01424 123456 (w) 01425 654321
email: rjjones@madeup.com

Experienced and mature design manager now seeking change of career into charitable sector. First class communication, presentation, and negotiation skills. Works well under pressure of deadlines and budgets. Great sense of humour and great team player, good at motivating and developing staff.

CAREER HISTORY

1992–2002	**Design & Production Manager**, Arco Publicity plc, London NW1. (Arco specialize in branding for SMEs, covering all aspects from concept to implementation.)

Role overview: to manage the Design & Production Department, producing all company literature, promotional and presentation media; to work with clients on timely and cost-effective design and production of literature, stationery, newsletters, web media.

Main Achievements

- steady growth of Department to turnover of £2.2 million from £0.5 million.
- attracting new clients with 90% client retention for more than 5 years
- building a cross functional team with high reputation for delivering on promises both to external and internal clients, after a period of stagnation in the Department.
- efficient setting and management of budget of £450K.
- creating company intranet and implementing its use, saving approx £15,000 p.a. on internal paper communications
- teaching departmental managers the fundamentals of design for inclusion in pitches to clients.

1992–1997	**Asst Manager**, Design Department, England & Son, Berkhamsted, Herts. (a small firm concentrating on delivery of design and printing to local clients). Left to advance career. *Role overview:* to manage the department's daily operation; manage small portfolio of clients; assist the Manager in budgetary control.

> Always include the headings of each section to make it easy for the reader to spot the information they need and to know what your CV is referring to.

> The emphasis on monetary and commercial achievements may be incorrect for a new career in charity. Stressing the team development and internal relations aspects might be more suitable.

Continued over page

121

	Main Achievements • motivating and encouraging the team through a period of recession and uncertainty • rebuilding client relations after several years of stagnation and poor standards • developing portfolio of clients • assisting in the merging of two Design Departments after the company bought out another local firm
1987–1992	**Designer**, Pop Promotions, London NW1 (a small company involved in promoting a variety of pop musicians). Left to advance career. *Main Responsibilities* included the design of promotional literature for pop concerts; presenting designs to promoters; liaising with printers and building up relations with them.
1983–1987	Freelance **Designer** working for a number of local businesses, designing and producing company stationery and literature. The recession made me look for financial security in a full time employed position.
1980–1983	Part time Office Manager at Allaboutdesign Co. I was able to use my free time to act as freelance photographer for Midwest Community Project, travelling to various events and photographing them for the Project's travelling exhibition and publicity material. The Project ended (as planned) in 1983.

EDUCATIONAL AND PROFESSIONAL QUALIFICATIONS
- 1977: 9 O-Levels, including Maths, English Language, and French
- 1979: 3 A-levels: Maths, Further Maths, and Design (all Grade B)
- 1983: Degree: B.Sc. Design, Keele University, 2.ii
- 1996: Chartered Institute of Designers, Post Graduate Diploma in New Media

EXTRA SKILLS: advanced IT skills in many design packages (including FrontPage, Quark, Dreamweaver), MS Office, email.
Good fluency in French through continuing use with one of Arco's clients

INTERESTS: Countryside and the environment—member of Ramblers' Association, National Trust, Worldwide Fund for Nature, Wildfowl & Wetlands Trust; blues music; family (married, two children).

REFEREES

John Arco, MD Arco Designs 76 Upper Street London NW1 020 7123 1234	Philip Johns (*personal referee*) 442 High Street Littletown Beds LU2 01442 123456

Richard and the manager at England & Son fell out, so Richard has not given him as a referee; instead he has opted for one good work referee and a personal referee.

Examples of covering letters

See Chapter 5. The following four examples show four types of covering letters. First, a standard covering letter from Joe responding to a newspaper advert for an office junior at a sports events organization.

---

47 West Street
Southampton
SO1

20 November 2002

Dear Miss Forbes

Re: Vacancy for Office Junior

I saw your advertisement for the above post in the Swansea Gazette and am enclosing my CV in application.

I have recently completed my BTECH and am now keen to start my career in a company which, as you say in your advert, can offer comprehensive training and experience in all forms of office administration.

As required by the advert, I have good IT skills (gaining a Distinction in this module in my BTECH) and have previous work experience in a similar role at a solicitors' office. I especially enjoyed the switchboard work this involved, and am therefore pleased to see this task has prime importance in your job description. As a fan of many types of sport, from football to snooker, I have an immediate interest in the main aim of the company and would be fascinated to learn more on the background of how events are organized.

I am available for an immediate start.

Yours sincerely

JOE SMITH

> It would have been more professional if Joe had also put Miss Forbes's name and address before the start of the letter.

Next, here is an example of a speculative application from Hannah, following up a lead given her by an ex-colleague.

Little Barn, Market Basing, Northumbria CA4

Mr E K Hammond
H R Department
Thomson & Legat plc
Unit 47 Business Park East
Carlisle CA2

20 August 2002

Dear Mr Hammond

Re: **<u>Vacancies in the Customer Services Department</u>**

Mrs Rachel Greening, Supervisor in the Customer Services Department, has informed me that Thomson & Legat are in the process of expanding this department and looking for new employees. I am therefore enclosing my CV and should be grateful if you would consider me for any suitable posts.

Following a career break while my children were young, I am now looking to return to full time work, building on my past 10 years' experience in Customer Service. As my CV shows, I have particular skills in:

- achieving high standards of customer service, with a demonstrable commitment to going the extra mile to improve the reputation of the company.
- learning products quickly. I have kept up my learning and self-organizational skills through studying for a degree while raising my family.
- telephone-based customer service
- database use to accurately log customer contacts to provide a full picture of the customer and form the basis of useful reports.
- supervising small teams

I understand that Thomson & Legat operate a flexitime system and this would be beneficial to my personal circumstances. This, and Thomson & Legat's renowned stance on customer service, adds significantly to the attraction of any career with the company. I am available for work after the 1 September 2002.

Yours sincerely

HANNAH MASTERTON

Hannah has not put in a desired salary: from her colleague she already knows these details and is happy with what the company can offer.

The next example is Kashmira, applying online for a management post.

To:	jjarvis@jarvisandjarvis.com
Re:	Translations Manager, Hansen & Koch
Atch:	KAtkinsCV.doc

John Jarvis
Jarvis & Jarvis Agency
25 East Cheap
London EC2

Dear Mr Jarvis

Re: **Translations Manager, Hansen & Koch**

In response to your advert in *The Bookseller* for the above post, I attach my CV in application.

A first class honours graduate in French and German, I am currently employed as Assistant Manager at the Andre Gide Translation Agency. I have been very happy here for the past five years but am now keen to put my management skills to greater use in a more demanding translation environment. The role of Translations Manager, as described in your application pack, seems to be an ideal position.

In support of my application I would note the following points:

1. Extensive experience in client liaison, building up good relations and developing new business possibilities with existing and new clients.
2. Strong management skills in team building through leading the team at Andre Gide during a long sickness absence of the Departmental Manager. I have dealt with a variety of situations from low staff morale to a case of absenteeism.
3. Sound budgetary experience, both setting and monitoring.
4. Respected translator of French to and from English in a variety of disciplines, often working to tight deadlines.
5. Good verbal and written communications, regularly contributing at management meetings, and writing for client and staff intranets.

When sending your CV on-line, call it more than 'CV' so that the recruiter can find it easily if they save it to their own hard disc.

Continued over page

Emphasize knowledge of the company and its reputation.

6. Excellent IT skills

7. Awareness of Hansen & Koch through their reputation in the industry, and a real enthusiasm to work for the company. The flat management structure and the emphasis on self-development is very attractive.

You state in your application pack that the successful candidate will be expected to take up their post in January 2003. I confirm that I would be able to meet this deadline, as I expect to move to London during the latter part of December.

Information requested by the agency: do not include unless it is.

I am seeking a salary in excess of £25,000, being currently on a salary of £23,500. Current additional benefits include private medical care and personal pension scheme.

I hope that the above is of interest to you and look forward to hearing from you. If you decide I am not suitable for the post with Hansen & Koch, please feel free to keep my details on file for future vacancies.

Yours sincerely
KASHMIRA ATKINS
Flat 6, 25 Manchester Street, Manchester M4
katkins25@btinternet.com

Finally, here is an example of how *not* to write a covering letter.

What's wrong:
- Failure to include a contact address
- Failure to find out the name of the right person
- Over informal style
- No mention of what job Mary's interested in
- Spelling mistakes
- Emphasis on what can be got out of the company

TO: the person in charge of recruitment

Hi!

My name is Mary Connors and I'm interested in any vacancies you've got. I'm attaching my CV so that you can see the skills and experence I have.

I'm really intrested in working for your company as it has a good reputation for staff development and training. Also, I've always been keen to work in your industry.

Hope to hear from you,

MARY CONNORS

Example of a completed job application form

See Chapter 6. Compare with Richard's CV on pages 121–2.

POST APPLIED FOR:	*PRINT & DESIGN MANAGER*
NAME	*RICHARD JOHN JONES*
ADDRESS	*THE MAPLES, RHOSNESNI,* *HEREFORDSHIRE HR26 2ZZ*
TEL NUMBER	*(h) 01424 123456 (w) 01425 654321*
EMAIL	*rjjones@madeup.com*
N I NUMBER	*PP 12 34 45 K*

EDUCATIONAL QUALIFICATIONS

9 O-LEVELS, INCLUDING MATHS, ENGLISH LANGUAGE, FRENCH AND GERMAN
3 A-LEVELS: MATHS, FURTHER MATHS AND DESIGN (ALL AT GRADE B)
DEGREE: B.Sc. DESIGN, KEELE UNIVERSITY, 2.II

PROFESSIONAL QUALIFICATIONS

CHARTERED INSTITUTE OF DESIGNERS, POST GRADUATE DIPLOMA IN NEW MEDIA

CAREER HISTORY

CURRENT OR LAST POST: give details of job title, employer, dates employed, main responsibilities, reason for wishing to leave or leaving.

DESIGN & PRODUCTION MANAGER, ARCO PUBLICITY PLC, LONDON NW1. 1992 TO 2002
MAIN RESPONSIBILITIES: MANAGE DESIGN & PRODUCTION DEPARTMENT, PRODUCING COMPANY LITERATURE, PROMOTIONAL AND PRESENTATION MEDIA; WORK WITH CLIENTS ON TIMELY AND COST-EFFECTIVE DESIGN AND PRODUCTION OF LITERATURE, STATIONERY, NEWSLETTERS, WEB MEDIA. LEAVING DUE TO REDUNDANCY.

Continued over page

Shows Richard has the right to work in the UK.

Insufficient room to list all qualifications so Richard has selected those most relevant to the post.

Note the form wants responsibilities not achievements, so Richard will have to include these in his reason for applying, if relevant.

Example of a completed job application form

PREVIOUS EMPLOYMENT

DATES	JOB TITLE	COMPANY	MAIN RESPONSIBILITIES
1992– 1997	ASST MANAGER	ENGLAND & SON	MANAGE DEPARTMENT'S DAILY OPERATION; MANAGE PORTFOLIO OF CLIENTS; ASSIST MANGER WITH BUDGETS
1987– 1992	DESIGNER	POP PROMOS	LITERATURE DESIGN; LIAISING WITH PRINTERS
1983– 87	FREELANCE DESIGNER	SELF-EMPLOYED	DESIGNING FOR CLIENTS
1980– 83	OFFICE MANAGER	ALLABOUT DESIGN CO	MANAGING DAILY OPERATIONS

ADDITIONAL RELEVANT SKILLS

IT: DREAMWEAVER, FRONTPAGE, MS OFFICE (ALL), EMAIL.

REASON FOR APPLICATION (continue on separate sheet if necessary)

MY MAIN REASON FOR APPLYING FOR THIS POST IS MY PERSONAL INTEREST IN THE AIMS OF THE CHARITY. COMBINING THIS WITH MY EXPERIENCE AND SKILLS IN MANAGING A DESIGN DEPARTMENT GIVES ME A THOROUGH UNDERSTANDING OF ALL THE POINTS RAISED IN YOUR JOB DESCRIPTION. (CONTINUED ON SEPARATE SHEET)

I confirm that the information in this application is correct to the best of my knowledge. I understand any attempt to falsify information will invalidate my application and/or any offer or employment.

Signed: ....

Date: ....

An easy spelling mistake to make!

The smaller space allowed for older jobs shows the company is less interested in these. Include only the most relevant responsibility.

Write your name and the title of the job you are applying for on the separate sheet.

Skills list

See Chapter 6, page 65. You may be asked to complete a skills list in an application as follows:

	No experience	Occasional use	Daily use	Qualified
MS Word			✓	
MS Excel			✓	
MS Access		✓		
Sage	✓			
Email			✓	
Internet				✓
Letter writing			✓	
Minuting		✓		
Purchase Ledger		✓		
Sales Ledger		✓		

If most of your ticks fall into the 'No experience' category, you are probably applying for the wrong job.

■ **Occasional use** or **knowledge of** means that you use this skill infrequently, or your skills are now rusty after a period of not needing to use the skill. Look for ways to brush up your ability.

■ **Daily use** or **working knowledge** means that you use the skill on a regular basis and require little training to carry out any tasks using the skill.

■ **Qualified** or **fluent** or **complete knowledge** means that you are thoroughly conversant with the skill and can use it with ease.

An alternative approach to a 'tick box' form may be for you to state your own level of knowledge against a list of skills. Use the terms above to demonstrate your understanding of each skill.

You could also use this approach on a CV, if you have many IT programs to list.

Checklist for internet research

Technology . . . the act of so arranging the world that we need not experience it.

Max Frisch

 Do!

look out for friends and acquaintances who are working for the company and ask them for their views.

 Don't!

call your friends at work and expect an in depth review of the company situation: ask them outside the work environment.

See Chapter 7, page 70. When conducting internet research on companies, you need to look for the following information. You might consider designing a standard form for yourself to complete (which is also good practice on form filling) and build up a database of information which you can refer to easily.

FULL NAME OF COMPANY	BEST NOISE MUSIC LTD
ANY PARENT COMPANY? IF SO WHICH?	JOHNSON MUSIC
HEAD OFFICE ADDRESS	25 East Street, Southampton SO2
ADDRESS OF BRANCH I WOULD BE INTERESTED IN	No branches
TELEPHONE	023 34983493
EMAIL	info@bestnoise.com
WEBSITE ADDRESS	www.bestnoise.com (www.johnsonbeats.com)
NAME OF PERSON WHO DEALS WITH APPLICATIONS	No name at Best Noise
NAME OF HEAD OF DEPARTMENT I AM INTERESTED IN	Don't seem to be departments at Best Noise
COMPANY'S MISSION STATEMENT/SLOGAN	'Making the best noise in the world'
ADDITIONAL INFO ON MAIN BUSINESS	Brings in new bands and brings them up to Johnson's level
WHAT'S NEW? EXPANSIONS, NEW PRODUCTS	Signed up 7 new groups whole of last year and have already signed 10 this year—expanding
ANYONE WHOSE NAME I RECOGNIZE ON STAFF LIST	I think Josh Miller, Administrator, was at school with me. Email and find out what he thinks of company!
NEWS ON COMPANY FROM OTHER WEBSITES	Lots of positive stuff on music magazine sites
CAREERS SECTION OF WEBSITE?	Best Noise says not taking applications till Jan. 2003
DATE APPLICATION LETTER SENT	15 January 2003
RESPONSE	Holding letter saying right person away on holiday: chase in 2 weeks time

Checklist for interview preparation

See Chapter 9, page 83.

- Reread the description of the job:

  - What are the skills you need to emphasize? How can you demonstrate these?
  - What experience is most relevant?
  - What queries do you have about the job? Make a list and take this with you to interview.

- Reread the company information:

  - Can you sum up the aim of the company in a few sentences?
  - What are the latest issues the company is involved in— expansion, reorganization, new products, etc.?
  - Who are the people who will be interviewing you?
  - What queries do you have about the company? Add these to your list of questions.

- Reread your own application:

  - Check what skills and experiences you have concentrated on. Can you expand on them?
  - Rehearse a coherent explanation of your career to date.
  - Rehearse a coherent explanation of why you want the job.

- Check you have everything you need to take with you:

  - directions for how to find the interview venue; phone number of company in case you need to call en route;
  - extra copies of your CV if asked for them;
  - list of questions to ask;
  - any examples of your work you have been asked to bring.

Quick Tip

If you have time and access, reread the company web site. What has changed since you first looked at it: new design, new information, latest news stories?

Logging your interview

See Chapter 9, page 92. When you return from an interview, take the time to record what happened. Again, you might want to design a form for yourself which you can refer to easily and use for comparisons with other interviews.

COMPANY NAME	*BIG NOISE MUSIC*
POST	*GENERAL ADMINISTRATOR*
DATE OF INTERVIEW	*2 DECEMBER 2002*
INTERVIEW VENUE	*42 EAST STREET, SOUTHAMPTON (NB THE ENTRANCE WAS IN LITTLE STREET!)*
WHO INTERVIEWED AND THEIR POSITION IN COMPANY	*MARCUS DIGBY—PROMOTIONS MANAGER, HELEN ABER—OFFICE MANAGER*
WHAT DID THEY ASK	• *WHAT I KNEW ABOUT THE COMPANY* • *WHAT MUSIC I LIKED* • *WHY I WANTED TO WORK FOR BIG NOISE (SAID PERSONAL INTEREST, GOOD SKILLS MATCH)* • *HOW I'D COPE WITH DIFFICULT PEOPLE, DEADLINES, PRESSURE* • *HOW FAST I LEARNED NEW SOFTWARE*
WHAT WENT WELL	*LIKED THE PEOPLE; THOUGHT I ANSWERED QUESTIONS WELL; THEY SHOWED ME ROUND*
WHERE I COULD IMPROVE	• *GOT THERE LATE BECAUSE OF THE ENTRANCE IN THE OTHER STREET!* • *DIDN'T FEEL HAD ENOUGH QUESTIONS TO ASK THEM*
ANY TESTING	*SHORT TEST ON OPENING UP THE INTERNET, FINDING WEBSITES FOR TWO GROUPS AND THEN INFO ON THEIR LATEST RELEASES. NO PROBLEMS.*
WHEN COMPANY IS TO CONTACT ME	*BY 10 DECEMBER*
FEEDBACK	*SECOND INTERVIEW 12 DECEMBER! WILL BE WITH MARCUS DIGBY AND SARAH JOHNSON (HR MANAGER OF PARENT COMPANY)*

 Don't!

ask questions for the sake of asking them at interview. You can always say, 'I'd thought of lots to ask but you've already answered them all!'

Other reward benefits

See Chapter 10, page 96. Employers can offer other rewards besides salary. Here are some of the more standard ones.

Pension scheme: by law, all organizations with more than five employees must give staff access to a pension scheme which employees can contribute to at low cost. What you need to think about is:

- how much the employer contributes to the scheme

- if your contributions are automatically deducted from your salary or if you can choose whether or not to join the scheme. If the deduction are automatic, what percentage of salary is this?

- whether the scheme terminates if you leave the company or if you can carry on contributing to it or even, if it is a personal pension scheme, if you can take it with you to the next job. Many companies will now contribute to the pension scheme of the employee's choice.

- if this is a company pension scheme, how it operates, what safeguards there are, and what say employees have in how funds are invested.

- what sort of payment and pension you get when you retire: is it based on a percentage of your final annual salary? Talk to a financial adviser for independent advice.

Bonus: check how bonuses are paid. Does the whole company have to reach a certain target, or the team, or you? How much is the average bonus? Will it be worth working under pressure for?

Commission: find out how commission is decided; is it a simple scheme or very complex involving too much paperwork to make it worthwhile? If several staff are involved in a sale, are there clear rules on how commission is divided up? Is commission paid annually, quarterly, monthly, weekly? What happens if a client cancels the sale—do you have to pay back

If you don't want to work you have to work to earn enough money so that you won't have to work.

Ogden Nash

133

the commission, and how? How much do other staff earn, on average, from commission?

Share options: there are a number of different ways a company can give you equity (shares) in it. You may qualify for free shares depending on length of service or you may be able to purchase shares at a reduced rate. Check how the scheme works and, again, take independent advice to ascertain how tax efficient the scheme is. You are liable to pay tax if you sell shares within a given period: check the terms of the deal and find out if you are actually increasing your tax bill.

Company car: a company may provide a car from its own fleet, or give you an allowance towards buying the car of your choice. Alternatively, you may be given an allowance for petrol or diesel. Each of these options has different tax implications, so as well as finding out what car you are offered, check you will not end up out of pocket.

Companies will only offer you this and the following two insurance benefits 'subject to underwriting'. This means if you have a poor insurance or medical history which makes it difficult for you to find insurance except at very high cost, the company reserves the right not to offer you these benefits.

Life insurance: companies may offer life insurance equalling twice or three times the salary being paid to the employee, a very useful benefit to anyone with dependants or if you have a mortgage. Check the amount being offered and what say you have in determining where the money is to be paid if you die. Many life insurance policies are dual policies offering **critical illness insurance** cover as well. This means if you are diagnosed with a terminal or very serious illness, the policy will be paid out to you on confirmation of the diagnosis.

Private medical care: as usual, you need to check the small print. You may have a scheme which is fully comprehensive, or only covers a given range of illnesses in a limited choice of hospitals. You can also see if your dependants are covered, or if you can purchase cover at a reduced rate for them.

Permanent health insurance sometimes known as **PHI** or **permanent income insurance**: this scheme pays out if you are off sick for a long period, usually over six months, though some schemes also activate after three months' illness. You will receive a percentage of your salary: not the full amount but more than you would under Statutory Sick Pay. Most schemes pay 75 per cent of your normal salary. Schemes may be index linked, meaning that if you are off sick for more than a year, the amount you receive rises according to the cost of inflation or a similar national index. Check when the policy starts: it would be a shock if you found the company paid you sick pay for three months only, and the PHI payments did not start until six months passed, leaving you with a financial hiatus.

Relocation expenses: if you need to move to take up a job, or if the company itself moves, you may be offered financial assistance with the cost of moving. Solicitors' fees and transport costs are usually covered by this benefit. Check the detail: if you get half way through buying or selling a property only for the deal to fall through, will the company pay the abortive solicitors' fees, or only pay on a successful transaction?

Subsidized mortgage: usually only available to employees with companies which offer mortgages. The company can provide mortgages at a reduced interest rate.

Interest free loan: the company advances you money for the purchase usually of a season travel ticket, with the amount divided into ten or twelve equal instalments, deducted from your monthly salary. It may be possible to borrow money for other items such as a rent deposit. Remember that if you leave the company before you pay off all the loan, the remaining amount will be taken from your final salary payment.

Accommodation: for live-in posts, free or subsidized accommodation may be provided. You will need to check what rules there are for bringing your own furniture, rules regarding families, pets, and visitors and what liability you have for repairs and decorating.

Crèche and other **childcare provision**: a major benefit if you have young children. Check whether the crèche is provided free or if there is a small charge; when it is open; how it is staffed. Companies may also offer vouchers to pay for nursery school places. You will need to see if your chosen school accepts the voucher scheme, and what effect on your salary

Other reward benefits

Keyman insurance is taken out by companies on workers who are crucial to the operation of the company. If the employee dies or is off sick for a long period, the insurance company pays the employer (not the employee) the equivalent of the salary of the key worker to allow the company to recruit and pay someone to do the job.

selecting vouchers has. For example, part of your salary may be paid in vouchers, which is not the same as being an additional benefit.

Holidays: current legislation states that all employees are entitled to a minimum of four weeks' annual leave, after they have been in employment for thirteen weeks. Annual leave may be pro rata if you are in a part time or fixed contract post which lasts less than a year. Check if the four weeks' leave includes bank and other public holidays, or if these are in addition.

Many companies now offer a sliding scale of annual leave, with increments being offered to long serving staff, or the option to take an unpaid 'sabbatical' leave lasting anything up to a year.

Employment legislation over recent years has introduced further sorts of leave such as paternity leave, parental leave and time off for dependants. However, legislation has mainly made these new types of leave unpaid, so if your company is offering any form of salary for these, this is another bonus.

Checklist for benefits

■ Read the small print: what are you actually getting?

■ For all financial benefits, take independent advice before signing up to any scheme. Find out what the tax implications are.

■ If a benefit is of no interest to you, such as childcare provision if you have no dependants, see what the company can offer as an alternative. With the growing diversity of many workforces, employers are open to a 'mix'n'match' approach to selecting benefits. However, you should note that this is generally confined to larger organizations and there will be no additional salary if you choose to waive a benefit.

■ Know your rights: don't be fooled into thinking something which the law obliges employers to give you is an additional rewards benefit.

Jobs outside the UK

Start with a visit to the official government web site of the country you are interested in working in. Most will have sections about employment for non-citizens and what visa and permits you will require.

Your route to employment will be:

■ through obtaining a job with a company advertising in the UK. These are either ex-patriate jobs offering tax-free salaries or through multinational companies looking to fill slots in offices in different countries. In this case you should apply as for a standard UK job. You will need to explain why you are interested in working outside the country, stress any language skills, and confirm any arrangements the company can offer for accommodation and dependants.

■ by travelling to the country and then starting your job search. Initial preparation is the key in this case.

- Think about contacting family, friends, and colleagues who have followed this course and take their advice on employment. What is the standard layout for a CV? How easy is it to find employment? What does accommodation cost?
- If you cannot find a contact with experience of the country, look for the web sites of recruitment agencies working there and check their advice and tips pages. You can also register your CV (or resumé as it is often called outside the UK) straight away online to give you a starting point to pursue when you reach the country.
- Work out financial arrangements: how much is a living wage? How much money should you arrange to have to tide you over until you find a job?
- Set up accommodation so that you are not left stranded at the airport with nowhere to go.

Workers holding a passport or identity card issued by any member state of the European Economic Area can work anywhere within EEA boundaries without needing an additional work permit. British Commonwealth citizens do not usually need a work permit to work in Commonwealth countries, but may need a visa. Check with your local travel agent.

If you are interested in voluntary work abroad, the VSO organization is a good starting place. You will be found accommodation and receive living expenses. Visit www.vso.org.uk.

If you are a non-British citizen and are interested in working in the UK, visit www.i-uk.com for comprehensive information on many aspects of living and employment.

Further reading and resources

Chartered Management Institute: 3rd Floor, 2 Savoy Court, Strand, London WC2R 0EZ. Tel. 020 7497 058. Web site: www.ocula. managers.org.uk/ institute/home

General

The Chartered Management Institute publish a series 'In a Week' focusing on various aspects of business skills. Similar series are published by the Chartered Institute of Personnel and Development.

Researching yourself

Chartered Institute of Personnel & Development: CIPD House, Camp Road, Wimbledon, London SW19 4UX. Tel. 020 8971 9000. Web site: www.cipd.co.uk

■ *Career Tests*, Louis Janda (Adams Media Corporation).

■ *A Manager's Guide to Self-Development*, Mike Pedler, John Burgoyne, Tom Boydell (McGraw Hill).

■ *The Which? Guide to Changing Careers*, Sue Bennett (Which? Books).

Researching the job

■ Directories of careers and companies are useful for giving you general ideas about which job would suit you. Try *The Times A–Z of Careers and Jobs*, Irene Krechowiecka (Times & Kogan Page) or *The Trotman Careers Directory*, edited by Kim Reynolds.

■ For information on specific careers, Kogan Page publishes a useful series called 'Careers in . . .' focusing on different jobs such as the police service, retailing, airlines, and airports. Kogan Page in conjunction with *The Times* also produces a series called 'Getting a Top Job in' various disciplines such as marketing, sales, and business development. Trotman publish a series called 'Q&A careers guides' on different jobs.

Researching the company

- *Hobson's Graduate Career Directory*, published annually, gives information on the larger companies. See also Hobson's web site, www.Hobsons.com.

- *The London Jobhunter's Guide*, published annually by Prentice Hall, gives information on London-based companies.

Online careers search
Books

- *Online Job Hunting* Martin Yate & Terra Darlain, Kogan Page

Newspapers

- www.jobs.guardian.co.uk: *Guardian*
- www.thetimes-appointments.co.uk: *The Times*
- www.jobs.telegraph.co.uk: *Daily Telegraph*

Recruitment sites

Look for directory sites of recruitment agencies and follow the links.

- www.reed.co.uk and www.hayesworks.com are two of the largest sites for commercial posts.

- www.charitypeople.co.uk for jobs in the charity and voluntary sector.

Dedicated job sites

- www.monster.co.uk
- www.fish4.co.uk/jobs
- www.workthing.com
- www.gojobsite.co.uk
- www.topjobs.co.uk for management and professional vacancies.

Trade press publications

- Jobs in IT and computing: *Computer Weekly*. Also online with www.cwjobs.co.uk

- Jobs in publishing: *The Bookseller*

- Jobs in television, radio, and film: *Broadcast*

- Jobs in food and drink, hospitality: *Caterer & Hotel Keeper*, *The Grocer*. Also online with www.grocerjobs.co.uk

- Jobs in charity: *Third Sector*, *Charity Week*

- Jobs in social care and welfare: *Community Care*

- Jobs in health: *Occupational Health*, *Hospital Doctor*

- Jobs in the holiday industry: *Travel Weekly*

Writing

Other books in the One Step Ahead series (see page 2).

The Oxford Guide to Writing and Speaking, John Seely (Oxford University Press, 2000).

CVs

- *The Perfect CV*, Max Eggert (Random House Business Books).

- *Writing a CV that Works*, Paul McGee (HowTo Books).

- *The Ultimate CV for Managers & Professionals*, Rachel Bishop-Firth (HowTo Books).

Interviews

- *The Perfect Interview*, Max Eggert (Random House Business Books).

- *Be Prepared! Getting Ready for Interviews*, Julie-Anne Amos (HowTo Books).

- *Best Answers to the 201 Most Frequently Asked Interview Questions*, Matthew J. DeLuca (McGraw Hill).

- *201 Best Questions to Ask on Your Interview*, John Kador (McGraw Hill).

- *Body Language at Work*, Adrian Furnham (Chartered Institute of Personnel & Development (CIPD).

- *Career, Aptitude and Selection Tests*, Jim Barrett (Kogan Page).

- Kogan Page and *The Times* publish a series called 'How To Pass . . .' focusing on different types of tests.

Jobs outside the UK

- Survival Books Ltd have a series called 'Living and Working in . . .' various countries.

- *Hobson's Guide to Careers in Europe*, published annually.

- *Jobs and Careers Abroad*, Dan Boothby (Vacation Work Publications).

- *Working Abroad: The Complete Guide to Overseas Employment*, Godfrey Golzen and Jonathan Reuvid (Kogan Page).

The other way round

If you'd like to know more about how HR professionals recruit, *Recruitment and Selection*, Gareth Roberts (CIPD), will give you inside knowledge.

Index